"Carmen LaBerge is a smart leader with years of experience in the trenches of church and culture skirmishes. In this book, Carmen challenges believers to view every person as an image bearer of God and to live each day in light of the redeeming love of Christ. We would all do well to heed that challenge."

—**Russell Moore, president of the Ethics & Religious Liberty Commission of the Southern Baptist Convention**

"*Speak the Truth* is a journey through culture with a wise guide. Carmen LaBerge brings clarity to the current chaos, by bringing all issues back to the one issue: God. I am thankful for her voice in the culture, and pray this book receives the wide reading it deserves."

—**John Stonestreet, president of the Chuck Colson Center for Christian Worldview**

"*Speak the Truth* is a wake-up call for Christians who have become complacent and fallen asleep in the pew. There is a world in desperate need of the Gospel and Carmen has written a book to both motivate and equip every Christian to bring the Truth into their own spheres of influence."

—**Donna VanLiere, *New York Times* bestselling author and speaker**

"While I had the privilege of serving in the U.S. House of Representatives for thirty-four years, I am under no illusion that the political process or political systems can solve all the problems our country faces. In *Speak the Truth*, Carmen LaBerge is calling people of faith to reject fear of engagement and live as God's ambassadors in a world desperately in need of hope and truth. This book is a straightforward resource for anyone who has been wanting to reenter the cultural conversations but did not know how. This book will equip you to understand the underlying issues in our culture and approach them with both grace and truth."

—Congressman Frank R. Wolf (Ret. 1981–2014)

"Carmen LaBerge is one of the most inspiring, energizing leaders of the Christian faith in our time. When she speaks, her words hold listeners in rapt attention, captivating them by the truth she imparts. When she writes, the words leap off the page and burrow down deep in the minds and hearts of her readers. In this marvelous volume, she incisively pinpoints the bankruptcy of modern secularism, and in response, she skillfully mines the richest treasures of Christ and our faith. Declaring that this is a moment of truth for America, she calls us as Christians to speak and live the ultimate truth—the truth of Jesus Christ. You will love reading, studying, and discussing this work from a master communicator of the Master's Truth."

—Howard Edington, preacher, pastor, and author of
The Forgotten Man of Christmas: Joseph's Story

"People enjoy talking, but not about everything. Most people don't talk about death. It's also often difficult for Christians to talk about God with people who aren't Christians. It isn't that they don't want to be helpful spiritually. It's because they aren't sure how to do it and don't want to offend the other person or fail to communicate effectively. In *Speak the Truth* Carmen LaBerge shows how to bring God into conversations and do it effectively. This is a practical, insightful book that will stimulate some powerful daily conversations."

—Luder Whitlock, president emeritus of Reformed
Theological Seminary and author of *Divided We Fall*

"Taking her cue from Jesus ('the ultimate angler'), Carmen LaBerge proposes that cocktail conversations become fishing trips. She encourages Christians to hook their neighbors 'with Kingdom curiosity' by catapulting otherwise superficial discussions onto a higher plane. The presenting subject is never the real subject, she says. 'Whether the issue is pancakes, porcupines, politics, or parenting, the issue is God.' In *Speak the Truth*, LaBerge offers helpful techniques for re-framing the discussion and introducing one's neighbor to Jesus Christ."

—**Parker T. Williamson, editor emeritus of the Presbyterian newspaper *The Layman***

Speak the Truth

SPEAK
THE
truth

How to bring God back into every conversation

CARMEN LaBERGE

REGNERY
FAITH

Scripture quotations are from the ESV® Bible (The Holy Bible, English Standard Version®), copyright © 2001 by Crossway, a publishing ministry of Good News Publishers. Used by permission. All rights reserved.

Cataloging-in-Publication data on file with the Library of Congress
ISBN 978-1-62157-634-1
e-book ISBN 978-1-62157-652-5

Published in the United States by
Regnery Faith, an imprint of
Regnery Publishing
A Division of Salem Media Group
300 New Jersey Ave NW
Washington, DC 20001
www.RegneryFaith.com

Manufactured in the United States of America

10 9 8 7 6 5 4 3 2 1

Books are available in quantity for promotional or premium use. For information on discounts and terms, please visit our website: www.Regnery.com.

Distributed to the trade by
Perseus Distribution
www.perseusdistribution.com

*This book is dedicated to the women who in many ways
I aspire to become: my mother, Ruthann Fowler Melzer, and her
mother, Rhobenia Ringwald Benefiel. My grandmother's wisdom,
dignity, perseverance, and love continue to bear the light of Christ
into the world through a legacy of faith that now extends to the third
and fourth generations. My mother's indomitable character, can-do
spirit, and winsome ability to discover and nurture the best in others
have provided a consistent vision throughout my life of an Imago
Dei woman. I would not be the person I am today were it not for the
maternal heritage with which I have been blessed. Mom, thanks for
calling me to a life of significance and for the example you have set
every day. You wouldn't be you if it weren't for grandma and
I wouldn't be me if it weren't for you. Thank you for leading me
to expect the unexpected and anticipate miracles, confident that
with God all things are possible.*

Contents

Introduction

Something is wrong.

America is divided over many things, but there is consensus that something is wrong. We may not be able to quite put our finger on it, and everyone from journalists to cultural commentators disagree over the root causes, but virtually every American recognizes our current state of polarization does not "we the people" make. Across the ideological spectrum we agree justice is not prevailing, tensions in cities are high, poverty has become the generational expectation for too many, fear is all too prevalent between neighbors and too many of our systems are working for too few. Globally, we acknowledge that America's credibility and influence have changed and political, sociological, economic, and religious finger pointing abounds. It's always the fault of *the other* and *the other* has become the enemy. There is no poetry in our politics and there is too much partisanship even among those who are supposed to be of one mind. Here I'm talking about Christians. That's right, I contend Christians should be leading the conversations in culture, bringing the mind of Christ to bear on the matters of the day, as ministers of reconciliation, not fomenters of greater angst.

So much is wrong that you may be saying, "where do we start?" Let's start with the first wrong. Let's start by acknowledging that at the root of every issue is the issue of Sin. Christians have home-field advantage when it comes to this conversation. Not only are we experts on the problem, we know redemption's remedy!

Let's go back to the good ol' days. We don't remember them because they were before our time. But there was a time when everything was right with the world. Before everything went wrong, everything was literally right. In the Beginning there was a rightness to life and relationship. People were right with God, right with themselves, and right with one another. Those were literally the good ol' days! So, no matter the issue of the day, the issue behind the issue of the day is the issue of Sin—and its solution: God's redemptive plan. People are already talking in moral categories of good and evil, and existential realities of life and death, purpose and love. But they are doing so without the necessary referent, God. So, how do we get people talking about what they're already talking about with the added element of God's perspective? *We* bring God back into the conversation.

Beyond Band-Aids and placebos that mask the pain for a moment but fail to address the systemic cancers of pride and envy raging among us, this book is an effort to get us talking together about taking our place in the revolutionary redemptive plan of God. We're talking about changing the conversation by changing every conversation. And that we do by getting God back into every conversation, every day.

Our culture is off its rocker because it is unhinged from its moral moorings. But who let that happen? Like everything today, that's debatable, but a good place to start is with a long look in the mirror. Could it be Christians stood aside while the eternal was disconnected from the everyday in America? Could it be Christians underestimated the effects of the appropriation of language, the co-opting of education and the yielding of institutions to atheistic ideologues? Somewhere along the way for many Christians in America, moral decision-making became something we judged by a set of criteria unhinged from God's Word. As norms aligned with God's revealed will disappeared, so too did the cultural cohesion necessary for the vision of a shared future. Without such a vision, people—as a distinct culture—perish.

When people know not God, they lose all sense of themselves. The identity politics dominating the selfie culture today is the consequence of a systemic identity crisis. As creatures, created in the image of God, but knowing not God, we cannot know ourselves. The confusion runs deep. Rare is the family today that does not have a son, a sister, a nephew, an aunt, or a parent whose preferred patterns of life depart to an alternative that is often systemically destructive to the family itself. Grief runs so deep and, yes, so does love.

We are facing an identity crisis as a nation, as individuals who do not know who they are, where they came from, why they're here, where they're headed, and what they're supposed to be doing have become the drivers of cultural conversations across many fields. Those who see the devolution for what it is have raised the alarm, but screaming ever more loudly at "those other people" when we catch them advancing the moral rot does not work. While I agree righteous indignation is a legitimate affect, vociferous anger is an ineffective technique for ministers of reconciliation advancing the Gospel. In short, angry is over in terms of Christian witness.

There was a time when I approached the issues, the threats to what I knew was right, with what I now see was less than love. Three shifts were necessary to arrive at the place where today I can genuinely engage any person about any matter with honest Truth in love. The three shifts were: one, seeing the person first, not the issue; two, asking God to give me His perspective on the person—and the issue; and three, recognizing my role as God's agent of grace, keeping a divine appointment God has set, for which God has an agenda, and in which God would be faithful to speak if I would simply submit.

I have learned that whatever the *presenting* issue, God is the issue. This person—no matter what adjectives are used to describe them—is a child of God and presently behaving like a two-year-old stomping a defiant foot at the Father. Whatever the presenting issue, the real issue is always the same. The brokenness of the self, division in the relationship, hostility toward righteousness, bad fruit—it's really all one issue: Sin. Once I remind myself this person is precious to God and currently living at enmity with Him, once I see the captive nature of a soul held as a prisoner of a spiritual war, my attitude and my approach is transformed. That's how God gets back into every conversation—by transforming and then using you and me.

If you are a Christian and your life of discipleship has been growing up in every way into Christ who is the head, then I'm hoping you're at the place where you see yourself as you really are and your calling for what it truly is. The Christian's job is to bear full witness to the beauty and truth of the Gospel today. To stand on the sidelines and scream your fool head off at the moral rottenness of your neighbor is a false witness to the way Jesus lived and the reason He died. If your first and continuing response to the moral revolution is bitterness, anger, and rage, then you may well need to sit a spell with Jonah before you seek to be God's prophet in today's Nineveh. Yes, God loves you, but God loves that person held captive by the Enemy as well. God's heart remains set on redemption. He's got you, now He wants them. Each of them and all of them. Not just the ones we like or the ones who are like us. *Those* people are the people God wants to redeem. So who is standing close enough to them to snatch them out of the fire? That would be you! The question is, do we have the Father's heart and the mind of Christ and are we ready to engage, by the power of the Holy Spirit, in the culture war of our day?

While things may be bad, relative to the places and times when others were called to bear this same Gospel witness, we have it so good! In America we have the liberty to believe. We are free to follow our Christ-formed conscience. We have a constitutionally guaranteed right to not only worship God in spirit and in truth, but to proclaim the Gospel to others and to bring our beliefs to bear in the public square. That is extraordinary! Enough with the whining. It is not working as a winsome witness and it is a distraction from our calling. It's time we looked earnestly to the pioneer and perfecter of our faith for how we might more faithfully serve Him as living demonstrations of the Gospel in the world today. Jesus did not sit on the sidelines of anything. He was on the move; He engaged every person He met as a divine appointment and every conversation was changed by His contribution to it. Even on those occasions where He was silent, Jesus spoke volumes.

If we're honest, we can admit Christians are guilty of raising the alarm every day about moral decay. But we have not been effective in actually stemming the flow of debased and debaucherous information into our own minds, homes or conversations. Christians in America have ridden the tide of moral debasement right along with the rest of the culture. Ever lowering the lowest common denominator with no end in sight. Yes, against that degradation we rage—but mostly among ourselves and often as hypocrites.

When we do enter the public facing debate, we give people a piece of our mind. Adding our own personal opinion to the cacophony of culture's current chaos. Is that what we're supposed to be doing? Is that the purpose for which we have been redeemed and sent as witnesses of Christ into the world? It is time to recognize and confess that something is wrong, not only in the culture, but in the Christian witness in the culture. The problem is not just "out there," it's "in here." The spirit of the world is in the churches of our nation and the spirit of division and self-promotion and self-interest are all too often operating in those who profess to be Christians.

It is time to come to terms with the truth that other people don't need a piece of *our* mind; what they need is the peace of the mind of Christ.

We often hear reference today to the "battle for hearts and minds." It is a statement about competing worldviews and it is open advocacy of the Western worldview in non-Western parts of the world. But the battle for hearts and minds rages right here in America as well.

Following the election and inauguration of Donald Trump as the forty-fifth president of the United States, there were riots and protests, the frequency, size, and scope of which had not been seen since the Vietnam era. The 2016 election cycle made clear that the "one nation under God, indivisible" was divided over many things. The Left thought it had won the culture war and then found out that tens of millions of Americans were, in fact, not convinced of their progressive, evolutionary, anti-family agenda.

One of the shifts that took place when the Trump administration replaced President Obama was that Christians were not only taken seriously, but welcomed into leadership. Christians who had been sidelined were suddenly front and center of the conversation on Capitol Hill, the Supreme Court, and in the White House. But culture isn't only made in Hollywood and D.C. Culture is made at every coffee shop, kitchen table, conference room, waiting room, and carpool line in America as Christians bring the Truth of Christ to bear always in all ways. And in order for that to happen, Christ has to actually be at the center of our thoughts, the very operating system of our minds, and the Spirit guiding our words.

The nominal approach that many self-identified Christians take to the things of the faith leave the world with good reason to not take us seriously about many other things. When Christians treat God as a blessing-dispenser, Christ as one counselor among many, and the Bible as anything less than what it really is (the very Word of God), the world is right to be confused and dismissive. The goal here is to not only declare anew the calling, but inspire anew the called.

The followers of Jesus Christ are all called to be His witnesses in the world right where they are, right now. The Christian calling isn't for someone else, to somewhere else, to reach someone else. The calling is for every Christian here and now. Yes, God calls some to be foreign missionaries to unreached people groups, but we must not fail to see that America is now a land quite foreign to the Gospel. Our call is here and our time is now.

Nearly a quarter of our neighbors and a high percentage of people in emerging generations now say they have no faith affiliation.[1] They are called the "nones." The society dominated by Christian institutions and thought in the 1950's now needs to be re-evangelized. The problem is few Christians are actually equipped to do that. Many self-identified Christians are not actually disciples of the One whose name they bear.[2] Some still hold membership in churches and some have titles and degrees indicating institutional church positions, but they really make their own way, design their own truth, and pursue their own version of the good life. Having neither the mind of Christ nor the Spirit of Christ, they misrepresent God, leading people to gross misunderstandings of who God really is. Their kids see through the hypocrisy and no longer have even the pretense of faith and their neighbors just think that's what Christians do.

Now is the time and this is the place for a distinctively Christian witness in America. It is time for a cultural revolution of redemptive grace in America.

It will not be bloodless revolution, but all the blood necessary has already been spilled by Jesus on the Cross. And while it is a war, it is not waged with the weapons of this world. Interim evidence of its advance will be marked in ways the world does not understand. But as good news is proclaimed to the poor, captives and the oppressed are set at liberty, the blind begin to see, we can be confident that the culture is being remade and transformed.

Transformed, yes; perfected, no. We know better than to expect utopia or heaven on Earth. That day will come, but until it does, life will be complicated and the Gospel will be contested. Indeed, this is the day the Lord has made and it is into this day the Lord sends us to bear witness to Him.

There is a culture war going on in this country and we can no longer remain silent on the issues affecting us all. But how do we engage in a way that honors Jesus? We are certainly not free to charge out into the world to slay people with our self-righteousness. Quite the contrary. Before we can move constructively into conversations as diplomats and representatives of Christ, we must first reject the reactionary responses and the spirit of divisiveness to which we have contributed.

Christians know and acknowledge there is one God and Father of us all; one Savior and one Way to salvation. We also live in a pluralistic society where ideas compete for the attention of thoughts and the affections of hearts. Living peaceably with everyone in a nation where everyone has the full freedom of their own conscience is a challenge worthy of the Gospel. As our society grows more racially, ethnically, ideologically, and religiously diverse this challenge presents itself in our cities, neighborhoods, schools, churches and homes.

A *Q Ideas* study conducted by Barna in 2014[3] reveals that most Americans believe "society benefits from having a diversity of opinions and viewpoints, because variety and debate lead to the best ideas and solutions for our common future." It also confirms "a healthy and vibrant democracy requires an engaged public—one that includes people of faith." As Christians we should not only celebrate the freedom of living in a pluralistic society, we should lead the conversations taking place in it.

So, why are many Christians standing on the sidelines of the cultural conversations of the day? Some will immediately protest that Christians are not on the sidelines, but loudly engaged in cultural debates in ways that certainly don't honor the Christ whose name they bear. That drives other Christians away from engagement because they don't want to be associated with a presentation of the Truth that is ugly and mean. Then there is the sideline crowd—huddled together with brows furrowed and arms crossed, scorning the very culture to which they have been sent to bear positive witness. Why? I can think of at least three reasons:

1. We fell asleep at the wheel.

Sometime around 1954 many Christians in America functionally went to sleep. Christianity dominated the institutions of the day so there seemed no need for vigilance. Teachers led prayer in school and taught from a distinctively Christian worldview. So, we figured, our kids didn't need us to intentionally disciple them. The church offered Sunday School and para-church organizations offered what the church didn't. The courts based decisions about moral behavior on Biblical principles. The media reinforced traditional Judeo-Christians values in everything from the Op-Ed pages of major newspapers to the nascent television and film industry. Things appeared good on the surface. Christian vigilance flagged as many turned their focus to self-interested kingdom building.

If you've ever drifted off to sleep behind the wheel you know the terror that dominates in the moment you awake. In an instant you must assess where you are and what needs to be done to avoid imminent death. That's how Christians feel when they wake up to the cultural realities of America today. They discover schools are teaching a world-view expressly contrary to Christianity. The courts are making rulings in express opposition to the Biblical worldview. And the media is saturating every moment of American life with dehumanizing, debased, coarse, foul, pick-your-adjective words, images, and storylines.

Things have changed and it is time Christians woke up to the reality that over the past six decades our culture was taken captive while we slept.

2. We're exiles in our own land.

The language, worldview, media, and conversation have changed so much we feel ignorant and ill-equipped to converse with those who claim to be intellectually and morally superior.

I have a confession to make: my language fluency is limited. I appreciate, value, and celebrate people who are fluent in more than one language, but my brain is wired for one: English. Communication requires two people sharing enough of a common language that what is said can not only be heard but understood. Gospel fluency today requires Christians to become fluent across generations, cultures, technologies, and the most rapid change ever experienced by any human generation. That's intimidating for the most well-equipped missionary and most of us have not been trained in cross-cultural Gospel fluency to reach people who are operating out of a completely foreign worldview.

3. We're afraid.

We're afraid of a world we no longer understand and people around us who no longer look, talk, dress, nor act as we think Americans "should." Fear leads to two predictable responses: fight or flight. The flight response is to self-isolate into what we hope will be protective enclaves where we can wait things out while someone else fights the culture battles and makes America great again (as we imagine greatness). This isolationist approach is detrimental in the near term, but its potentially devastating down the road. If Christians self-isolate, insulating the next generation in the hope of protecting them from all the evils of the world, they will be utterly unprepared to take their stand when the time comes.

The other response to fear is we fight—and fight we must. But we do not fight with the weapons of this world. We answer cursing with blessing. We answer hate with prayer. We answer those who come after Jesus, not by reaching for the sword, by reaching out hands of restorative healing. In the Garden of Gethsemane, Peter reached for a sword and hacked off the ear of a Roman guard. But Jesus transformed the man, healing him. Our job is to bear witness to Him. Our job is to let Jesus do what Jesus does—transform human lives by restoring people to right relationship with the God who Is, even if they reject Him and those who represent Him today.

The culture is being influenced continuously to change. If you are not influencing it to change for the better then however others are intentionally influencing it will determine its course. We influence the trajectory of culture in a myriad of ways, but the simplest is to cultivate the mind of Christ on the matters of the day and then bring that mind into the conversations we have with others—particularly those different from us. The generational divide is one place to start but that bridge requires thinking in ways you may not have thought before.

We must admit that we don't quite know how to engage with the emergence of self-focused morality.

According to the *Q Ideas* study,[4] 47 percent of Americans reject the idea of moral absolutes. That means nearly half of our neighbors don't see a fixed difference between right and wrong. So, how do we present the reality of a sovereign God who is the moral lawgiver, the origin and the summation of all things, and whose Son, Jesus Christ, is the only way to salvation to people who largely reject the notion of objective truth? "Jesus loves me, this I know, for the Bible tells me so,"[5] doesn't cut it when the Bible is not regarded as authoritative. And the idea of commandments, submission, obedience, self-denial, sexual restraint and calls to holiness are a hard sell for a nation of people who are immanently morally flexible and insatiably self-interested.

To this we add the basic fear that comes from being on the defensive and in retreat. The militant sexual culture warriors have largely succeeded in bullying academics, artists, politicians, and the judiciary into seeing sexual liberty as a right that usurps religious freedom in the United States. To be a conservative Christian today—or even a Christian who is orthodox in their belief and practice—is to be open to the charge of extremist, bigoted, closed-minded, ignorant, out-of-touch, behind the times, or on the wrong side of history.

To this issue let me say: fear is not faithful. At least not this garden variety fear. It's time for Christians to get a grip on the truth that the Church is persecuted. There's not part of the Church being persecuted and some part not. *The* Church, the body and the bride of Christ, is persecuted. It always has been and it always will be—until it's not.

If you're a Christian in this day and age it's time to get a grip on reality. This isn't Eden, it isn't the Promised Land and it isn't anywhere close to Heaven on earth. But this is the day the Lord has made and this is the time and place into which God has called us as the ambassadors of the Kingdom of Heaven amidst the kingdoms of this world.

So, how do we engage the culture in a way that honors Jesus?

The short answer is conversational apologetics. That means helping others reconnect the eternal with the everyday by walking with them the distance from where they are to where the conversation that's directly about God begins. Think of it as pre-evangelism. It's all the work that has to be done to an untended, littered, parched, weedy patch of earth prior to actually planting a garden.

Google "urban garden" in the news. What returns did you get? Are you familiar with the reality of food deserts in inner city America? Are you aware of the urban garden movement? Can you see the Gospel in it?

Take a piece of inner city America and turn it into a garden that feeds the local community with good things. Yes, you have to start by removing the trash and yes, it's laborious to till dirt that's been lying under concrete for a generation. Yes, the soil has to be enriched. Yes, you have to dig down deep. Yes, it takes time and attention and effort. But when people taste and see that the Lord is good—when the sun rises and the rain falls and God gives growth, when the harvest is abundant and feeds the body—then the soul begins to catch a glimpse of the beauty and truth of the Gospel. My alma mater, Princeton Theological Seminary, actually now has a Farminary program. Why? Because come to find out there really is something about a garden that is intrinsically true. There really is something about the teachings of Jesus relevant to people who aspired to be post-agrarian. Can you make that connection? Could you take your sun hat and your gardening gloves and pull weeds today in an urban garden? What conversations might be had? What relationships might be cultivated? What fruit of love, joy, peace, patience, kindness, goodness, generosity, and self-control might flower? How might you—and maybe someone else—be renewed in hope and faith across what currently divides?

Remember Jesus' walk to Emmaus? He came alongside and joined two people as they walked the seven miles from Jerusalem to Emmaus. He observed their distress and grief. He inquired about their conversation and He stopped and listened to them. He asked an open-ended follow up question and listened to their answer. Then, having listened, he started to talk. He reframed the entire conversation. He gave them the Biblical worldview on the issues of the day. He helped them see things from God's perspective. Their hearts burned within them and eventually, their eyes were opened and they recognized the Truth that sets men free. They ran the seven miles back to Jerusalem to share the good news with others and Jesus showed up to resolve any doubt and "open their minds so they could understand." You can read the entire amazing account in Luke 24.

Seven miles is a long way to walk in the desert on a hot day. With whom are you walking today in order that they might talk about their confusion, disappointment, and grief? Are you opening the Scriptures with them as a part of those conversations? Is Christ being revealed to them in the bread you break in fellowship? This is what mission work looks like in America today and you're the missionary whom God has appointed to serve in whatever stretch of dusty road you happen to find yourself on.

Jesus entered conversations that cut across cultural barriers—He spoke with women and children and tax collectors and Roman sympathizers and Pharisees and prostitutes and fisherman and lepers and paralytics and blind beggars and teachers of the law. He did not regard Himself as out of place in any place and He did not regard any person as an issue. And as soon as we protest, "Well, He's Jesus!" we belie the fact we don't quite know what it means to live a Galatians 2:20 reality: "I have been crucified with Christ and I no longer live, but Christ lives in me. The life I live in the body, I live by faith in the Son of God, who loved me and gave himself for me."

You and I cannot engage the culture in a way that honors Jesus if we do not understand that the life we are living is not really our own. Jesus is using the vessel of our body, our life, here and now, to advance His own Kingdom's purposes. We are the tool. We are the instrument. The Spirit is His, the words are His, the agenda is His. If at any level we continue to think it's about us—that we are the ones being rejected by the world, that we are the ones being humiliated—then we still have some dying to do.

People often ask me, "How do you know what to say?" The truth is, I don't. But it's not about me.

> God knows the person who is before me in this very moment.
>
> God knows the circumstances of their conception, the scope of their prenatal care, the reality into which they were born.
>
> God knows whether or not they were read to and nurtured as a child, the language and entertainment to which they were exposed. He knows if anyone ever took them to church.
>
> God knows the challenges they've faced, the pain they've suffered, the secrets they hide from everyone else, the self-conscious tapes running through their mind.
>
> God knows how they feel when they stand naked in front of a mirror, the wounds that formed their scars internally and externally, and what they fear.
>
> God even knows what they dream, but dare not hope.
>
> God knows things I could never know and even if I had all the time in the world, I could never learn. So in this moment of time we have together, in this moment of divine appointment only God could set, I trust God knows how to speak His redemptive love into their life.

Knowing God knows them, I confirm that God knows He's got me. "God, I know you've got this person in your heart and in your sight. Take my mind, my heart, my mouth and use me."

In that two sentence prayer I commit anew to know nothing but Christ and Him crucified for the person before me. I admit I do not know whether this is the first tilling of the soil of another human heart or the seed being planted or the watering of the Spirit or the pruning of the gardener or the opportunity for a harvest of righteousness. God alone knows what He has in mind for this particular divine appointment. The less I think about myself and my own inadequacies the better. I am but a mouthpiece, an ambassador, a representative, a conduit, a servant. Jesus is the One who loves this person before whom I sit or stand. Jesus is the One who, by the present power of the Holy Spirit, tenderizes my heart and conforms my conscience and forms my thoughts and gives the words. All I have to do is trust God to be God and submit.

Does that lead to ridicule and rejection? Sometimes. But so what? I don't particularly care what people walk away thinking of me. I care deeply what they now may be thinking about Jesus. If I've done my job, they're thinking about the possibility there is a God and He knows them and wants to be known by them.

The one-off encounters with those we meet along the road of life may be easy by comparison to being Christ to our neighbor. The more sustained relationships are the ones where we may have some "make up" work to do. We share a fence-line or a hedgerow or a wall and we have a catalogue of complaints about how they live. They know we are Christians but not by our love. We've frequently given them a piece our mind, but rarely (if ever) have we given what they actually need: the peace of the mind of Christ.

Each of us needs to admit there are those relationships in which our claim to represent Jesus has been compromised by the way we've done so. We've presented the gospel in ways that are not Gospel. We've said things in the name of Jesus, Jesus would not say in ways Jesus would not speak. So, our task here is largely about *how* we engage the culture in a way that honors Jesus.

In His sovereign desire that all the world should know the grace offered in Jesus Christ, God has set divine appointments for us to keep every day. When we miss them, the conversation carries on without

God's perspective being brought to bear, the secular humanist world-view goes unchallenged and an anti-Christ worldview is reinforced. It's time for Christians to get back into the conversation, not so we can give people a piece of our mind but so they might have the peace of the mind of Christ.[6] It's time to put God in His place, back where He belongs, in the middle of every conversation. To do that, God's people have to get off the sidelines and in into cultural conversations of the day. So, let's get started!

QUESTIONS FOR PERSONAL REFLECTION AND GROUP DISCUSSION

1. What is the difference between addressing issues and addressing people?
2. Do you celebrate or condemn the pluralistic nature of America? Why?
3. Of the reasons listed, which one best describes why you're on the sidelines of some of the cultural conversations of the day:
   a. I fell asleep and I'm just waking up to the reality that America needs to be evangelized.
   b. I feel uninformed and inadequately equipped.
   c. I have a fear of being rejected, called names, or hated.
      Now, discuss why you feel the way you do and how you think the Lord could make use of you anyway....
4. How do you understand the concept of conversational apologetics?
5. What is one issue (or person dealing with an issue) you hope to be able to better address after reading this book?

CHAPTER 1

Where God Belongs

His name is Omran. When his home was bombed in August 2016 he was five years old. Omran does not have a conscious memory which was not formed in the context of war. *Seeing* him changed America, if only for a moment. Do you remember seeing him? He was sitting in a sterile ambulance. He was covered in soot and blood. He sat motionless. His eyes were fixed straight ahead, his little hands resting in his lap, his chubby bare feet extended toward us, blood visible through the layers of bomb debris on his left temple. He was not crying. He was not screaming. He just stared, at no one and at everyone. And we stared back, our minds wondering what in the world the world had come to.

One little boy in America didn't just *look at* Omran, he *felt for* him. His heart went out to him. He empathized with Omran and he did the only thing he could think to do. He asked the president of the United States to go and get Omran and bring him to his house.

Like the little boy in New York we instinctively know *this* child in *this* circumstance—*this* is not how it's supposed to be. *This* is not what childhood is supposed to be. *This* is not how people are supposed to live. *This* is not how conflict is supposed to be resolved. *This* is not how God intends things to be. Ah! Therein lies the reconnect. Until our minds arrive at this question, we are simply rummaging around in the disconnected, situational, pragmatic ethics of our age.

In response to every Omran, every headline, every crisis, we ask, "what is God's perspective on *this*?" What does *this* look like from heaven? What is the Kingdom position and the King's posture on *this* person and their plight? God certainly sees and cares and God intervenes in order to keep His eternal plan on its redemptive track. Which is where the question for the Christian gets personal. God cares. Do I? Am I seeing this through the Father's eyes—*this* child, *this* war, *this* world? As His Kingdom ambassador right here, right now, how am I called to engage all *this* in a way that honors Jesus?

Omran was born in Aleppo, Syria in the midst of an uncivil war. Diplomacy failed and the Syrian government and Russia laid siege to Aleppo in September 2016. The dead were not even counted. Once the largest city in Syria, Aleppo now lays in utter ruin. Her people slaughtered by their own government. And we watched it happen.

By the time of the bombing of Omran's house, half of the people of his country had already fled the fighting. Half. One of those who fled was Alan Kurdi. Do you remember him? He was the three-year-old Kurdish boy whose body washed up on the beach after he drowned in the Mediterranean Sea.

While this is not a book about the refugee crisis, war, human suffering, resource allocation, jihad, nor our responsibility for our fellow human beings—it is a book about all these things and every-thing else. Why? Because God is as interested in Omran and Alan as He is interested in the children whose names we know, birthdays we celebrate, and futures we insure. Those children you comforted, fed, worried about, bathed, dressed, played with, prayed for, and tucked in before you sat down in the safety and freedom of your own home to read this might have been Omran or Alan.

We may have seen their pictures dozens of times, but I want you to think back to the first time you saw them. When Alan's lifeless body on the beach or Omran's piercing visage appeared on your Facebook or Twitter feed the very first time, what went through your head and heart? Did your prayers arise? Did your heart go out? Did your mind wonder? Mine did. I wondered, *who is this boy? What happened? Where is this taking place?* And the question, which pierced my soul: *Why is he all alone?*

Months later, we learned more about Omran and his family. Without getting into all the details, his story has been used by oppos-ing sides in the Syrian war, treating him and his family as pawns in a geopolitical war.[1]

There are now answers to many of these questions, but let's press the conversation beyond the surface. Beyond what we're looking *at,* what are we meant to see through the Father's eyes?

- We are looking at a fellow human being, a person. What does this mean? What is personhood? What is the value of a human life?
- We are looking at a human life shaped by war—what does that mean for the individual and what does it mean for life together?
- In Omran's case, we are looking at a boy who one day will know we knew. He will know we knew the day his brother suffered injuries resulting in his death and he

will know we didn't rush to his aid. He will know we knew the forces of evil at work raining fire upon his homeland and we did not send our own forces of good to do battle. He will know we knew the circumstance of his life and he will know we knew his name.

The desperation of the parents in these stories breaks the hardest of hearts. What wouldn't you do for your children? In the offer of the boy from New York can you hear the echo from eons past when the Father said to the Son, "Go get them and bring them home"? How does that change your perception? As those who represent Christ in the world today, we speak the Good News into the darkness by understanding the times in which we live and bringing God's perspective to bear. In order to do that we have to know both the times in which we live and the heart of God.

Thinking back to the day I saw Omran's face for the first time, an individual in one of my social networks posted the photo of Omran and captioned it, "war is hell." Another posted the same picture with a three-letter statement: "OMG." Do you recognize each of those captions as an opening for a conversation? The people who "friend" us on Facebook and "follow" us on Twitter have invited us to speak into their lives. The choice we make as individuals is whether or not—and how—to engage.

As a Christian, as an ambassador of Jesus Christ, as God's representative in this particular conversation, what do I say?

Yes, war is hell, but the reverse is also true, hell is war.

And yes, crying out to God, declaring my heartbreak at the horror of this little boy's plight is a legitimate response, but is OMG so overused as to be a meaningless form of prayer?

There is a war, a battle, being waged over every human heart and mind, in every generation. There's a war being waged right now over the territory, terrain, contours, and sovereignty of your life. There's a battle for your attention, your affection, your thoughts, your words.

From the Beginning there has really only been one question: me or Thee? Who gets to be Lord of this one life? Who gets to be god of my thoughts, the god of my relationships, the god of my affections, the god of my education, the god of my internet habits, the god of my finances, the god of my medical decisions, the god of my perspective, the god of my words, and the god of my deeds? In every moment you and I (and every other person in all the world) are making one choice: me or Thee?

Granted, the overwhelming majority of people are not consciously thinking about any of this. They are making decisions on the fly, based on their gut reaction, in whatever they perceive to be their own best interest—and in that, they betray the truth and bear witness to the me-centeredness of life. In a word, it is idolatry of the self. We know in our heads God belongs at the top of the list of priorities and His rightful place is on the throne of our hearts, governing our thoughts, sovereign over everything. But as human beings we must also acknowledge the head competes in every moment with the selfish urges of our desire for comfort and whatever we perceive as right in our own eyes or expedient for our own good.

When we hear or read the headlines of the day, the question is often asked, "Where was God?" The Christian must speak up and give assurance that God hasn't gone anywhere—in whatever joy or triumph, devastation or adversity you face, God is. That is His nature and He will not act in ways inconsistent with His character. So, in every moment it is relevant to consider: what is God's perspective on *this*? Because His thoughts are not our thoughts and His ways are not our ways, we have to be trained to see and think and respond as God would. We do not naturally have the mind of Christ on the matters of the day. It must be spiritually cultivated.

This I know, Jesus would be *in* the picture with Omran. The layers of anguish in the picture are many. I hate that he was born into war. I hate that his brother died. I hate that all he knows is hiding and shelling and suffering. But what haunts me is that in the photo, Omran appears to be all alone.

Not one person in all the mayhem is in view to hold him, comfort him, assure him everything is going to be okay. Everyone is attending his own needs and no one, at least in the moment captured in the now iconic image, is attending to Omran. Does Omran know God loves him? Does Omran even know there is a God with whom there is perfect peace and in whose Kingdom war will be no more? Who will tell him this Truth? Who will incarnate to this little boy the reality of the God who is, the God who cares, the God who has come, the God who redeems life from Hell itself and the many hells we endure during this life on earth?

We can be sure that in the battle for hearts and minds someone is speaking into Omran's life right now. Just like our kids, someone is filling his mind with ideas and heroes and dreams. The ideas being planted in his mind and reinforced by his experience have consequences. If you think your contribution to a conversation doesn't matter you are wrong. Every day which passes without our actively speaking into the lives of children, we are surrendering that fertile soil. Someone is speaking to their hearts. Someone is planting ideas in their heads. If not Christians then who?

Turning to an issue in our culture, consider the confusion created when our kids do not know how to discern truth from lies and the damage done by encouraging them to listen to all kinds of voices without ever attuning their hearts and minds to the voice of God. An article appeared in *Sojourners* on the subject of coming out.

The author self-identifies both as a Christian and as bisexual. She then proceeds to reveal the confusion wherein the pre-fall Creation of humanity in perfection is presumed to be preserved post-fall. Being careful here not to criticize the person, let us seek to engage what she has written. The author writes:

> But my God is love. And I believe that God is bigger than what my conservative church background taught me.[2]

Indeed, God is love, but love is not God. To say love is God and then to describe the love being elevated as a particular physical erotic expression unaligned with God's intentional and blessed design is idolatrous. It is however refreshingly honest, to hear the confession that love is really the god being worshipped by those seeking the affirmation of LGBTQ lifestyles.

You may protest, observing that the author acknowledges God is the Creator saying:

> God is my Creator, and God does not make mistakes.[3]

This is absolutely true. But the writer states this fact in an effort to claim God's blessing upon a proclivity that is beyond the pre-fall declaration of good in Genesis 2. Which leaves us on the post-fall side of things. Here on this side of the fall, people are conceived in, born into, and touched at every level by the reality of Sin. There is no part of us that does not need redeeming which is why the entirety of who we are—including our sexuality—is covered in the transformation received by those who become new creations in Jesus Christ. The old—all of it—is gone and the whole person is made new. Spiritual rebirth is necessary because the way we are born is Sin-full.

Let's continue in conversation with the author's confession:

But then there's also the issue of bisexual erasure. As I've considered coming out, I've also realized that bi-erasure exists. I experienced it in action. Sometimes I feel like I have to convince myself that I'm actually real: Gay people rarely talk about bisexual people; straight people usually focus discussions of sexuality on gays and lesbians. Allies tend to forget about us. I mean, being bi is just a big old hot mess sometimes.[4]

What do we have here? From earlier exposure to people who identify as bisexual it is my understanding that what is surfaced here is a sense of invisibility. If you think about it, this should not be a surprise. When a bisexual person is with a partner of their same sex they are seen as homosexual. However, when a bisexual person is with a partner of the opposite sex they are seen as heterosexual. How then do they present themselves in order to be seen as bisexual? The author rightly acknowledges "being bi is just a big old hot mess." What she misses is that the big old hot mess is the identity crisis of sexual confusion, the idolatry of self-expression, and the god she has made of love.

Confusion has a cause and part of that cause is the voices we allow to influence our thinking. If, at any point, the voices to whom you are listening are at odds with the Word of God, you should allow Christ to take those thoughts captive and you should actively confront the lies masquerading as truth. With that in mind, read what the author reveals about the voices she has allowed to influence her thinking:

But I keep hearing from others that telling our stories is the way to freedom. I keep hearing that sharing our testimonies is how we grow and change, connect and love. I keep hearing LGBTQ people say that coming out was the best thing they ever did. I keep hearing that hiding and pretending is harmful, dangerous and unhealthy. I keep hearing that it's so much better to be real and live out your identity.[5]

Telling self-focused stories is simple idolatry. It is not the way to freedom, but further into bondage. Jesus Christ says the truth is what sets us free. As Christians the best thing any of us ever did is accept the free gift of God's grace in the redeeming and reconciling sacrifice of Jesus Christ. Any other assessment of "the best thing they ever did" is like the false advertising of beer sellers who say "it doesn't get any better than this." Lies are lies no matter how pretty the packaging or how good they make us feel.

I absolutely affirm the author's declaration that God loves her and God wants her "to live as a whole person, not as a partial person, or a deceptive person, or a fake person." And I want to say to her, "bisexuality is not the wholeness you seek but in fact a deception and falsehood that will leave you forever feeling divided in your love, in your loyalties and in your life.

"There is no question God made you, God loves you, and God offers to bring you into full conformity with His desire for your life as you give up who are in order for Christ to live in and through you. But here's the rub: He's not so much interested in *your* sexual gratification, *your* personal fulfillment, nor whether or not *you* get the periodic rush of cresting an emotional roller-coaster. He's interested in the glory of God and advancing the Gospel of the Kingdom always in all ways. Living in alignment with that God and in community with those people is a total rush."

Not excommunication but extra communication

Finally, it must be noted what the author admits craving is community. Those who constitute and represent Christ's body in the world today, those who are ambassadors of the Kingdom and agents of grace must not shun but engage individuals who are confused and afraid. Instead of excommunication we need extra communication. We need to walk toward, not away from, those who misunderstand the nature of fallenness, the pervasive nature of depravity, and the reality of the Gospel.

If we allow false narratives to go unchallenged, we are contributing to the advancement of a kingdom which is not Christ's. We're either actively working at the Cross' purpose or we are working at cross purposes to the Cross.

God is not an ornament added to life or a mythical comfort created out of human imagining. God is objectively real, a personal reality who not only makes life possible but redeems life as actually good. And this we know because, by grace, through faith, in Jesus Christ, by the power of the Holy Spirit, we know God. That is extraordinary!

When we live as if God is not, we betray the Truth. To deny God's reality and God's sovereignty is a lie we know we're telling. That is what Paul calls active suppression in Romans 1. And we actively suppress the truth every time we leave God out of a conversation where we know He has something to say.

Back to Omran and Alan: If war is hell, then we should be sure people also know hell is real. And we should let them in on the reality that there's an Enemy of their soul hell-bent on keeping them in the dark on a path of destruction toward a destination which is literally hell itself. Don't want to sound kooky? Don't want to be "that" person? "Consider Him who endured from sinners such hostility against Himself, so you may not grow weary or fainthearted" (Hebrews 12:3). Reset your eyes on Jesus and remember anew who He is, what He has done, where He now sits, and what He has planned. Then look again at the person from whom you are considering concealing the Truth.

To conceal from others the truth and grace of God's reality, His love and the hope He offers in life and in death may well be the gravest sin we ever commit. If it breaks our hearts Omran has lived his entire life on earth in the context of war, do we care if most people we meet every day are going to spend their *eternal* life in the reality of hell itself? If war is hell then let's see it as such and say so. When the world uses the word, let's be sure they know what it means.

But here we must pause. Do we actually believe in hell? According to a LifeWay/Ligonier study in 2016 for many the answer is "no."[6] We have, by our own admission, become a nation of make-believers, believing what we want to believe in a cobbled together iFaiths of our own liking. That, my friends, is idolatry, not biblical nor Christian by any recognizable definition.

The revolution of redemption is not just needed in the culture, it is needed within us. The work of salvation is fully accomplished, but we are not yet fully conformed to Christ. That process of sanctification—becoming holy as God is holy, is the essence of discipleship. It is a moment by moment process that takes a lifetime. Make no mistake, I'm not talking here about a transformation confined to the spiritual. Life in Christ is a comprehensive reorientation that includes acknowledging God's presence, power, and purpose in every experience.

We don't actually have the power to put God in His place, back where He belongs, but as God is restored to His rightful place in our lives, our perception of His presence, power and persistent counsel changes. God is not moved but we are.

> As we see God more clearly,
> walk with God more closely,
> honor God more fully,
> yield to God more completely,
> yearn for God more deeply,
> respond to God more readily,
> we begin to speak of God more openly.

The One we long ignored becomes our audience of One whose attention and affirmation we crave. He becomes the one-and-only affection of our hearts, the be-all and end-all of our lives. We desire to know His thoughts so we might walk in His ways. We no longer toil to make a name for ourselves, but to make the name of God known to others. We give up our own kingdom building to seek first His Kingdom.

God is thereby restored to His rightful place in our lives, right where He belongs, in the middle of everything—including every conversation. When God is at the center of our thoughts, when He comprises the content of our character, the goal of our labor, the head of our household, the Lord of our health, the ruler of our internet practices, the master of our politics, and the subject of our conversations, He's right where He belongs.

The reverse is also true. When God is relegated to the periphery or the backseat or the sideline, we are living as if we have the power and authority to boss Him around. This puts us right back in the Garden in the original contest of the wills between me and Thee.

That's where the contest for control started, in the Garden. Rebellion against God and His perfect design is nothing new. It can feel like the current cultural power struggle in the so-called culture wars to pull us away from a Christ-centered perspective are newly powerful, but when we pull back the curtain on history we see otherwise. We have been attempting to replace God or conform Him to our own image since very nearly the Beginning. And even when we think our generation has found new ways to do it, we are reminded there is nothing new under the sun. Things (and behind those things, people) were at least this bad in the days of Noah when "The LORD saw that the wickedness of man was great in the earth, and that every intention of the thoughts of his heart was only evil continually" (Genesis 6:5). The next verse tells us it grieved God's heart. It still does. It's hard to imagine the days of Noah were worse than the realities described in

Judges 19 and Jesus says the days of Noah are coming again before He does (Matthew 24:36-37). The teacher in Ecclesiastes is right again, there is nothing new under the sun.

Confusion about gender roles, orientation, and identity? Not new.

Confusion about life and death and resurrection? Not new.

Confusion about race and religion, pluralism and relativism? Not new.

Cultural contests between man and God in terms of sovereignty, governance, justice, and care for the poor? Not new.

God cares about all of it and if God's perspective is missing from the conversations about these and every other matter it's not because God is silent, it's because we are.

I started it

Back in 2006, *Time* did something different for "the person of the year" award. Based on the explosion of the Internet and the ability of each individual to create content, *Time* said "You" are the person of the year. Facebook was only a few years old at that point, but already, we recognized anyone could have a following. And, the self-obsessed concluded everyone was entitled to be an American idol with an audience.

Not so many years later, "selfie" was Oxford Dictionary's official word of the year. Selfie sticks became a thing. Perfecting the selfie to achieve the highest possible number of likes or shares is consuming the attention of an entire generation. No longer interested in the grandeur of the Grand Canyon or Niagara Falls, the selfie culture wants to focus on themselves in the forefront and foreground of every moment. The height of this self-centered arrogance is captured perhaps best in the perverse trend of taking selfies at funerals. Yes, that's a thing with a dedicated website. If at another person's funeral you're trying to make it all about you, well, you have missed the point.

The selfie mindset is fooled into thinking reality is that which is self-filtered, cropped, and enhanced through a lens of personally defined truth. The all-important "I" is at the center of every moment captured and communicated from our preferred perspective. In our American context particularly, where the rights of the individual are now exalted above the common good in many ways, self is exalted as the one to whom everyone must bow. The problem is that we are an utterly insufficient point of integration. We were never meant to be at the center of it all. Again, this is not really new, the self-focus, self-promotion, and self-identification we see across our social media pages is an age-old problem on a new platform.

While we may be finding new applications for idolatry, the good news remains: God is. Colossians 1:15–20 tells us:

> He is the image of the invisible God, the firstborn of all creation. For by him all things were created, in heaven and on earth, visible and invisible, whether thrones or dominions or rulers or authorities—all things were created through him and for him. And he is before all things, and in him all things hold together. And he is the head of the body, the Church. He is the beginning, the firstborn from the dead, that in everything he might be preeminent. For in him all the fullness of God was pleased to dwell, and through him to reconcile to himself all things, whether on earth or in heaven, making peace by the blood of his cross.

He is Lord of all and He is reconciling to himself *all things, whether on earth or in heaven.* Quite literally everything. Total sovereignty. There is not one thing outside His reach and not one person outside of His concern.

It is humankind—not God—who has sorted pieces of life into sacred and secular. Into what is "His" and what is "ours." Church on Sunday morning—God time. Football on Sunday afternoon (and Monday night and all day Saturday)—mine. We imagine we're giving God His due by showing up on Sunday morning when God's due is all we have, all we are, and all we do.

We treat life like Monopoly. When we land on a square God "owns," we owe Him rent money. He can have those certain properties, but as far as the rest of the board goes—we pursue it for all we're worth. Truth is, it all belongs to God and at the end of the game of life, it's all going back in the box. We are fooling ourselves to think otherwise.

We like to think there's no connection between the sectors of life and by sectioning off topics as sacred and secular we can retain control over what we submit to His Lordship and what we hold out as our own. Just to be clear, that's not how it really works from God's perspective. You're either His or you are not. With Him or against Him. Either Christ is Lord or you are. No shared throne. The Hebrews called it the Shema and Christians call it the first and greatest commandment and it is this: love the Lord with all your heart, all your mind and all your strength. Emphasis on *all*. Comprehensive submission. Total surrender. My all in all.

The Bible makes it clear ultimately God reigns and ultimately every knee bows. Philippians 2:8–11 announces, "that at the name of Jesus every knee should bow, in heaven and on earth and under the earth, and every tongue confess that Jesus Christ is Lord, to the glory of God the Father."

God does not leave us to wonder how the story ends. He tells us in plain language. It ends with Jesus on the throne and every single knee bowing in full submission to His authority. We either humble ourselves now or we will find ourselves humbled. Those who do not know Jesus read that as a threat. Those who know Him read it as a great comfort because we know in letting go and yielding to God the peace which passes understanding and the power of the Holy Spirit and the hope, which never disappoints, become ours.

Submission is a dirty word in our "selfie" culture. The very notion that a person would give up their autonomy, identity, and control runs counter to our culture. But submission is simply acknowledging the truth—God is God and we are not. It is granting to God His *actual* place as Creator and King.

If we want the good life then we need to know what is good. To know what is objectively good we must know the One who alone is good. But knowing God means a radical reorientation of our lives. It means a new heart, a transformed mind, a subordinated will and a life brought into conformity with Christ.

With that transformed perspective on ourselves and everything else, we are compelled to engage with others around us. We see people in one of two states: in bondage to sin and death, prisoners of the Enemy of God, or reconciled to God in Jesus Christ and thus free, even if in bondage in this world. We become spiritual warriors, yes, but the battle is different than our worldly minds imagined. We find that we are agents of grace and ambassadors of a King from a Kingdom without end.

So the question is not "Does God give a damn about Omran?" The question is do we see Omran as a person equally worthy of knowing and experiencing the reality of God's grace and the hope of heaven as our own kids? If he's still alive and he's still in Syria, then he's still living in the reality of hell on earth. That rightly horrifies us. But do we honestly care that every person who does not call on the name of Jesus is facing the prospect of hell for eternity? This life is a fleeting breath by comparison.

We need to make an honest assessment of our own worldview and whether or not we have the perspective of God on the matters of the day.

The need for people, even religious people, to step back and evaluate their worldview is not a new exercise. In Matthew 16:1–3 Jesus noted the same inability, among notably religious people, to discern what God was doing in their day.

> And the Pharisees and Sadducees came, and to test him they asked him to show them a sign from heaven. He answered them, "When it is evening, you say, 'It will be fair weather, for the sky is red.' And in the morning, 'It will be stormy today, for the sky is red and threatening.' You know how to interpret the appearance of the sky, but you cannot interpret the signs of the times."

Suffice it to say Jesus did not perform for them a party-trick miracle-on-demand. Reducing God, or God's Son or God's Spirit, to something with whom we can toy or control or use is a persistent problem. We cannot seem to escape the captivity of our own time, our own limited experiences and concern for our own welfare. Although God certainly loves us personally, God's concerns extend to every other person in every other place as well. We cannot fathom that but it's true. God's thoughts are not our thoughts and God's ways are not our ways. He sees the whole world and everyone in it. And He shows no particular partiality. He's not so much obsessed with today as He is with the full scope of redemptive history. So, although the Gospel includes personal salvation, that alone is a gospel too small.

The Gospel is personal and the Gospel is global. The Gospel is for you and me and this nation and the Gospel is for people who speak thousands of different languages, live in places we will never see, have no education, live in squalor, were married off as children, sold as trafficked slaves, wander the world as refugees with no nation to call home, are addicted to opioids, homeless, jobless, convicts, and have the same and only hope of salvation: Jesus. The Gospel is the solution to jihad in the Middle East and the Gospel is the answer to famine in

Africa. The Gospel confronts human sex trafficking in Asia and resolves the secret loneliness of your single neighbor. The Gospel is neither aligned nor held captive by any particular kingdom of this world but inaugurates a Kingdom that will never end.

That's the Good News of the great Gospel we're in the world to proclaim. The only thing keeping us from doing what God has told us to do is pride. We don't want to embarrass ourselves. We don't want people to close their eyes, wag their heads, and take us off the list of people who are going to be invited to the next tailgate or cookout. God forbid!

If we're proclaiming the whole Good News of the Gospel and not some reduction of it, then people will be drawn in. But we must engage in the conversation in a way that honors Jesus. How do we rise above the condemnatory way the Gospel has been presented and instead, re-present the grace of God in all the fullness of its beauty and truth?

It starts with a revolutionary reorientation inside each one of us that leads to a redemptive revolution all around us. As we go we put God back where He belongs at the center of our own lives. He then makes His way naturally into every conversation in and through us so the Gospel might be extended to more and more people. That's His big plan and that's our part in it!

QUESTIONS FOR PERSONAL REFLECTION AND GROUP DISCUSSION

1. Me or Thee. What does that mean to you?
2. In what area of life (thoughts, words, deeds, affections, relationships, attitudes, etc.) have you moved God to the sideline? Are you willing to allow Him His rightful place as Lord?
3. War is hell. What does this mean to you?
4. What pricked your conscience as you read this chapter and how can you imagine the Lord wanting you to respond?
5. Who is one person God brought to mind as you read about the prospect of the reality of eternity in hell? (Ask the group to pray for you in the relationship and how you can relay the Gospel.)

CHAPTER 2

God, Muted?

Not everyone had a mom like my mom, but everyone needs a mom like my mom who speaks truth with integrity into your life. Whenever something failed to get done that needed doing, my mom would remind my sister and me of the Whobodies. It was a story that went something like this:

> Once upon a time there was a family of Whobodies.
> Their names were Everybody, Somebody, Anybody,
>   Nobody.
> Everybody noticed something needed doing.
> Somebody told Everybody to do it.
> Everybody said that Anybody could do it.

Anybody thought it was Somebody's job but Somebody left
  it to Anybody.
In the end, Nobody did it.
Everybody was upset because Nobody did what Anybody
  could have done and Somebody should have.

My mom never had to articulate the moral because by the end of
the Whobody recitation my sister and I were already silently negotiat-
ing who would be doing what Anybody could do. We knew that
Everybody was considered a Somebody in our family. We were the
Whobodies and we had been put on notice. The recitation ended
thusly: "Everybody pays the price if Nobody does what Anybody
could do and Somebody must. In this family, Everybody is a Somebody. So, figure out which of the two of you is going to do it because
if Nobody does it, Everybody is going to wish Somebody had."

The household of God version of the story has a twist: Jesus is the
One and Only Somebody who could transform Nobodies and Any-
bodies into Somebodies so Everybody could become a part of the
Whobody family of God. Jesus makes us Somebodies and then sends
us to Everybody who is still living as an Anybody or a Nobody with
the message of the Gospel.

Christians are the Somebodies who, by the power of the Holy
Spirit, bear the reality of Jesus Christ into the world. Call it what you
will: ambassadors, agents, representatives, spokespersons, witnesses,
mouthpieces, instruments, conduits—the reality remains, those who
call on the name of Jesus are the Somebodies who constitute the Body
of Christ in the world today. That body of believers, also known as
the Church, is charged with one mission: the Gospel.

When I ask an audience to call out the name of the foreign country where they'd most like to be sent as an ambassador, hands immediately shoot into the air. People either choose a country they know
well and love or they choose a country where they've never been. This
always intrigues me. I ask, "So, you do not know the language, the

form of currency, the customs or the political climate and yet you want to be an ambassador. What's your plan?"

To be a faithful and fruitful ambassador one must not only love the homeland and be an advocate of its values, worldview, and government, but one must also love the people of the country to which you are sent. Every Christian has been sent to serve as an ambassador of the Kingdom of Heaven amidst the kingdoms of this world. Most reading this have been sent to serve in the United States of America. We are not only responsible to represent the King of kings and the Lord of lords, to talk about and long for the Kingdom from which we hail and to which we will return, but we must love with deep affection the people of the land to which we have been sent.

The United States is a mess. The litany of what's wrong is long, and cultural commentators talk at length about how government can make it right. I have news for you; the issues confronting the United States (or any nation under heaven for that matter) are not going to be solved by secular government alone. Change is needed, but to misplace hope in any earthly king or kingdom is an error Christians must not make.

Christians can live distinctively and authentically Christian lives under any form of temporal government. In the United States we are privileged to be living in a context of religious freedom, but most Christians around the world do not. We are privileged to be living in a nation whose foundations are constructed upon morals and ideals derived from the Bible. Most of our brothers and sisters around the world, most of our fellow citizens of the Kingdom, are not. Does God love them any less than He loves us? No way and in no way! To suggest God loves Americans more than people of other nations is to bear witness against the over-identification of Biblical Christianity with any particular state, including the United States.

What the world needs is not a Christian America but for the Christians in America to be distinctively and authentically Christian. If everyone in the United States who claims to be a Christian were living an authentically Biblically-informed, Christ-redeemed, Spirit-filled,

Kingdom-advancing life, the culture would be transformed. Perfected? No. Without issues? No. But it would be perceptibly different in positive, God-honoring ways.

I mentioned last chapter that LifeWay research did a project for Ligonier in 2016. It revealed the heretical state of theology in America. It shows that although an overwhelming majority of Americans love the Bible, they know little of it. They love God, but have no relationship whatsoever with Him. Strange love.

The research reveals the nation is not only Biblically illiterate, but theologically confused. Here are a few research findings that demonstrate how comfortable Americans are with religious beliefs that are not only incompatible, but contradictory:

- While 70 percent say there's only one true God, and 66 percent believe God is perfect and cannot make mistakes, 64 percent also say they believe God accepts worship of all faiths and 60 percent either agree or are not sure if modern science discredits Christianity.
- In one place in the survey, 54 percent of respondents say only those who believe in Jesus will be saved but in another place 60 percent say everyone eventually goes to heaven—suggesting there's no need for a savior.
- In one place, two-thirds of Americans say they believe Jesus is God, but in another place 50 percent say Jesus is a created being. Americans are equally confused about the third person of the Trinity. Fifty-six percent say the Holy Spirit is a force rather than a person.
- The confusion about these matters stems from the confusion over the Bible. Fifty-eight percent of Americans say God is the author of the Bible but 51 percent also say it is open to each person's interpretation as he or she chooses.[1]

Let's consider that for a moment. If what the Bible says is "open to each person's interpretation as he or she chooses" then the Bible could mean anything. If the Bible can mean anything then the Bible means nothing because it is no longer an intentional communication of God to Man.

When it comes to the conversation about the Bible's application to life, suffice it to say the research reveals a deeply disintegrated worldview when it comes to sin.

- Sixty-one percent of Americans believe God is concerned about our day-to-day decisions, and 65 percent believe God has authority over all people because He created human beings. But then only 50 percent believe the Bible (which 58 percent believe is God's word) has the authority to tell us what we must do.

Questions relative to the church reveal:

- Fifty-five percent of Americans are comfortable with churches retaining the moniker of "Christian church" even if they do not preach from the Bible.
- Seventy-one percent either disagree or are not sure if local churches have "the authority to withhold the Lord's Supper from me and exclude me from the fellowship of the church."
- Fifty-four percent say "the church should be silent on issues of politics."[2]

So, half of the nation thinks God should be put on mute. Me, not Thee. Every cultural driver, from the media and academia to law, science, medicine, technology, foreign relations, and mainline denominations leave God completely out of most conversations. And yet we know God is not silent.

The fact that God speaks is established throughout the testimony of the Bible. Genesis 1:1 opens with "In the Beginning, God said." The Gospel of John opens by confirming "in the Beginning was the Word and the Word was with God and the Word was God." The book of Hebrews likewise opens with the confirmation of God's spoken revelation. Hebrews 1:1–2 reads, "Long ago, at many times and in many ways, God spoke to our fathers by the prophets, but in these last days he has spoken to us by his Son."

We know God and His Word are immutable. He never changes. James 1:17 tells us, "Every good gift and every perfect gift is from above, coming down from the Father of lights, with whom there is no variation or shadow due to change." And Hebrews 13:8, "Jesus Christ is the same yesterday and today and forever." This means He does not lie and what He says is good—forever.

But we know by our own experience that individuals can and do turn a deaf ear to God. Likewise, a culture can functionally mute God by suppressing what He says, preferring to satisfy their itching ears with their own collective worldly wisdom. This is the state of things in the nation where we have been deployed to serve as ambassadors of the Kingdom of Heaven. We are now the representatives of Christ and we are charged with living as Kingdom citizens and echoing what Christ says about what the Kingdom of Heaven is like in *this* kingdom context.

As soon as I say God could be muted, there are those who will rightly push back arguing "God is God and over Him people have no effective power." True, but to put your phone or your TV on mute does not mean the source on the other end has stopped broadcasting or stopped speaking, only that you—by a deliberate act of your own free will—have stopped listening. The message of the sender is not getting through because the intended recipient has covered their ears. God, muted.

Humanity has a long history of hitting the mute button on God. We've literally been doing it from as far back as we can collectively remember. When the father of lies entered the story of Creation and perverted God's good command restricting the first people from eating of the tree of the knowledge of good and evil, the people might have called out to God to intervene or they might have repeated word for word what God said. They did neither. Relying upon their own ideas and the new ideas being offered by the Enemy, an interpretation of the Word of God and thereby a mischaracterization of God emerged. That led down a path of destruction many still wander today.

However, God and His redemptive plan are not without their witnesses. That is the role of the Church in the world and, by extension, the role of every Christian.

You often hear Christians in America assert that God has been sidelined primarily because the secular culture pushes the Biblical worldview from the table of public discussion. This feeling is understandable when secular thought seems to control so many of the institutions of influence. The protest from the religious right is "America is no longer a Christian nation." The burden of that condemnation rests not on the culture but on the Christian. It is the Christian's responsibility to break into the conversation with the diplomacy of an ambassador, as an agent of Grace, speaking the Truth in love.

Christians have largely lost the sense of themselves as ambassadors of the Kingdom of Heaven to the kingdoms of this world. God deploys Christians as His ambassadors around the globe and this nation is our particular diplomatic post. We are resident aliens with dual citizenship, but we should never become confused about where our true allegiance lies. We are in the world, but we are not a part of it. This is not our home. We're here on a mission on behalf of another King and another Kingdom.

When you consider the identity, posture, role, and responsibilities of an ambassador, look in the mirror and address yourself appropriately. Put your shoulders back, raise your chin, speak as one who has dignity and authority. Live into your calling as a representative of Jesus Christ in the world today. That is who you are. That is your mission—should you choose to accept it. And therein lies the rub.

Too often, too many of God's people shrink back from conversations when we should lean in. Some suddenly recognize they're in Enemy territory, look down and see they failed to put on the full armor of God (Ephesians 6), turn tail, and run. Others have to admit they're pretty rusty in terms of the actual handling of the Sword of the Spirit (the Word of God). But the vast majority are so busy with the things of this world they don't perceive themselves to have time for the Divine appointment God set. In the end we must admit we just don't really care that much for the human Nobody currently before us. We sit in judgment like Jonah or we pass by on the other side en route to something more important to us.

If that's not bad enough, there's another equally prevalent problem: we engage the conversation, but we do so in a way that fails to honor Jesus. We give people a piece of our mind, which bears no resemblance to the mind of Christ. Failing to represent Christ accurately, we misrepresent Him in ways that leave negative impressions of the King and the Kingdom. In terms of diplomacy, that's a failure left to be addressed by another Kingdom ambassador who has to fix the mess we've made.

The deep divisions we experience as a nation statistically populated by a majority of Christians bears witness to the fact we don't know what we're doing in terms of living out the Gospel. The mind of Christ is not divided, so why are we? The Unity of the Spirit produces a bond of peace, so why are we at open warfare with one another?

I contend God's perspective has been sidelined because His ambassadors have conceded their role in the conversation.

Some readers will immediately push back on that, arguing that Christians are very loud and very prominent in today's cultural conversations. They scream and point and condemn. I would suggest the manner of their representation is actually bearing false witness. They are not engaging the culture and its people in a way that honors Jesus. You cannot present the Gospel in all its beauty and truth in ugly, mean-spirited, angry, violent, or non-redemptive ways. That kind of witness ought to be thrown out of the diplomatic corps by those Christians who understand that our public and private witness to Jesus must be aligned with the mind and spirit of Christ Himself lest the witness we bear be found false by the Judge. God forbid the name of God be blasphemed among the people of our day because of us (Romans 2:24).

Here is a practical example: boycotts. The next time you hear a call to boycott a business for taking a position contrary to the Bible, take a moment to consider all the options. While sometimes con-science demands we just cannot shop or support a business due to an immoral or unethical practice, using our purchasing power to bully businesses may or may not be what a foreign ambassador should do.

In the nineties, boycotts were a regular part of Christian activism against corporations supporting the "gay agenda." I would argue we missed an opportunity to do the work of having conversations with our neighbors about God's good design for marriage and sexuality. Now, gay marriage is accepted by a majority of Americans, is the law of the land, and companies fear the financial repercussions for *not* supporting the cause du jour of the sexual revolution.

Now, to be consistent and boycott *every* company with policies or positions against the Bible, Christians would have to give up drinking soda, shopping at most big-box stores, and watching pretty much all TV because of the advertising. Sporting events, subsidized by advertis-ing from boycotted companies, would also necessarily be forbidden. Following this logic, we might as well just withdraw completely and create our own alternative reality. Boycotts have proven strategically impactful but the fact that we are inconsistent across all sectors and in relationship to all sins, leaves our witness compromised in the world. Perhaps instead of cordoning ourselves off we might consider leaning into conversations with those with whom we disagree.

Yes, the cultural currents of secularism are rising fast against us, but that's no excuse. We are the generation of Christians whom the sovereign God of all redemptive history saw fit to send today. This is our day and this is the day the Lord has made. We are the particular, peculiar people whom God saw fit to send "for such a time as this." So, let us stop wringing our hands and waiting for Anybody else to arise and do what Nobody is doing. It's time to be the Somebody who makes the world different by bearing the presence of Christ into the world.

For our image-rich culture a picture is often worth a thousand words. The picture is that of a quickly crafted cross—two broken pieces of rubble lumber lashed together with fraying twine. Carried on the shoulders of war-weary men back to the top of a thousand-year-old church where the bells stopped ringing two years prior. The town is Bartella, Iraq. The offensive is the push-back against the Islamic State. The soldiers are not Christians. But the value of the Assyrian Christian witness has been so consistent and the blood of the martyrs so saturates the sands that they wept in replacing a cross atop the place from which everyone knows the only hope for civilization flows.

Juxtapose that with the picture of U.S. mainline churches covering their crosses or removing them altogether so as to not offend Muslim refugees from the same region. While here some would seek to mute God, the Church in other parts of the world is crying out from the very sands of time. In many ways we are more akin to the Christians in Iraq than we are akin to the nominally church-going people in America today. The sense of Kingdom citizenship and global kinship with Christ's people in China, the Middle East, former Soviet nations, and Africa will invigorate our own witness as we learn to stand up and speak up here and now.

LifeWay Research did a study on American Christians' willingness to share their faith in 2012. They found 80 percent of Christians who attend church at least once a month agree they *should* share their faith. But 61 percent had *not shared with anyone* how to become a Christian in the last six months.

Then, another LifeWay study found Americans who do not attend church are actually quite open to talk about faith with friends. Seventy-nine percent agreed with the statement, "If a friend of mine really values their faith, I don't mind talking about it."[3] This should be an encouragement and a warning to us. But, that same research found churchgoers would rather talk about politics than God!

If our relationship with Jesus is integral to who we are, then it is only natural to talk about it with people in our lives. This is a completely different approach than one-off conversations lecturing people about what they should or shouldn't do or how they should believe. The research begs us to shift our perspective from monologue to dialogue.

Looking further in this research, there was one particularly startling data point. LifeWay asked, *How concerned are you about people in your neighborhood who have different spiritual beliefs than you?* Americans generally are not concerned. This is not a surprise in a pluralistic society like ours. We value the freedom of others to worship and believe as they want, or to not believe, without fear or prejudice.

But looking specifically at those who have evangelical beliefs within the study, 51 percent were not concerned about their neighbor's spiritual beliefs. That's troublesome. If we do believe we have the good news of eternal life, but are unconcerned about others missing out, what does that say? Are we missing the key element of compassion for our neighbor?

It is time to "unmute."

God desires to use us—people who have a restored relationship with Him—to bring His perspective into the conversations of the day. We are regular run of the mill, ordinary Christians—"God's people," sent out to speak as ambassadors of His Kingdom perspective. That will mean we must learn to counter the false testimony of those who speak their own mind on the matters of the day misrepresenting God's character or His viewpoint. The spirit of the world is in the American church which means we not only have to speak the truth in love to the outside world, we have to call out error within the household of faith.

God calls us to walk in the Spirit and keep in step with Him. That means that the life of the Christian is not passive. We are the active agents of a God who is on the move.

I think of it as three steps: incarnational, relational, and transformational.

Incarnational: being an ambassador is your identity

The word incarnate means in the flesh. Jesus, the eternal second member of the Trinity, became incarnate (took on flesh), dwelling among us, fully God and fully man, with the purpose of making God known and atoning for Sin through His substitutionary death on the Cross. We learn a great deal about God's character from Jesus. We learn to glorify God by observing and listening to Jesus. When Christ comes then to dwell in us by faith, in the power of the Holy Spirit, we become the physical bodies through whom Christ is making His appeal to others: be reconciled to God. The idea we now have a role in Christ's incarnational ministry is mind-blowing. We are His hands and feet and mouths in the world today. When people encounter us, God's plan is they would be encountering Christ.

That means every moment is an opportunity to demonstrate the beauty and truth of the Gospel to others.

Don't panic. I know that can sound really intimidating, but remember, it's not "me" that is doing this—it's the power of Christ at work within me. I am in Christ, a new creation, a temple of the Holy Spirit, abiding in God, bearing good fruit. So, it's me, but not me alone. It's me, filled with the Holy Spirit, in league with millions of other Christians likewise filled, empowered, and sent. I'm responsible to faithfully keep the divine appointments God sets for me on any given day. You're responsible to faithfully keep the ones He's set for you.

As we've said, conversational apologetics is more pre-evangelism than direct evangelism. It's walking with people in the midst of the realities of life and getting them to think from a different perspective, God's perspective. We don't always have to overtly say that. We're tilling soil, removing rocks, planting seeds, watering sprouts. God gives the growth. Don't feel like you have to "seal the deal." Most conversations do not end with a confession and prayer of repentance unto faith. The One who seals the deal is the Holy Spirit and He is moving actively always in all ways. Our job is to keep step with the Spirit—not getting ahead of God and not lagging behind, but step by step attentive and responding to His leading.

Incarnational witness is as much seen as heard; and as much overheard as heard. Praying at meals in public settings is one simple tangible example of this. Christians give thanks over their meals. That's pretty much Discipleship 101. But there are times that Christians forgo praying over the meal in public settings. Why is that? Are we afraid of offending people but unafraid of offending God? Are we trying to be sensitive to the people sitting with us, around us, or serving us?

Try this: when we are dining out, after we've met the person who will be serving us and ordering the meal, there's usually a lull during which the server comes to check on us assuring us that our meal will be out shortly. We like to take that opportunity to share with the server (whose name we have been intentional to learn), "We're going to pray before our food arrives. Is there a specific way that we could pray for you or something in your life?" The offer has NEVER been refused. Sometimes the person has to leave, gather their thoughts and come back, and as of the writing of this book, we've never been declined. It doesn't matter if you're eating at Cracker Barrel or Ruth's Chris, the people serving food are often not treated as precious image bearers of

God who have eternal value and dignity. What if your treatment of them in offering to pray for them could begin to redeem that?

When we pray, we pray out loud but not loudly. We pray for the concern shared and we give thanks for the food and the hands even now preparing it. We also intentionally ask that "Christ may be made known to others in our breaking of the bread." In this prayer we center ourselves and are mutually reminded that everything we say and do in public is a witness.

At the end of the meal we assure the server of our ongoing prayers and we leave a generous tip. That too is a witness. If you have to order less food to leave a generous tip then do so. Put the concern of the laborer ahead of yourself in this tangible way.

Relational: ambassadors live among others as representatives of another Kingdom

Relational witness acknowledges Jesus didn't just take on flesh and then die an atoning death, He lived long enough among us to provide a faithful pattern of relating to God and one another.

Whether you look inside your own family or into the nation at large, you see the world's need for redemptive relationships. Yes, each person needs a redeemed relationship with the Father and that comes through a relationship with Christ alone. But people also need examples of redeemed marriages, redeemed parent-child relationships, redeemed friendships, redeemed political relationships, and redeemed relationships between nations. That too is our job as Christ's ambassadors in the world today.

This might be a shocking news flash but you were not actually redeemed by Christ for your benefit only. Yes, Christ died for you, but the Gospel is a whole lot bigger than that. The redemptive plan of God does not, in fact, revolve around you. It revolves around God.

God is internally and externally relational. God is relational as Father, Son, and Holy Spirit, and in Creative Redemptive history, God is relational with everything and everyone He has made.

God relates to His creation at all levels and God cares deeply about that which He has made. That means our relational witness is not just about our relationships with Christians, non-Christians, parents, spouses, siblings, children, friends, coworkers, and neighbors. Our relational witness is about people who live in places we will never visit, under circumstances we are loath to imagine. And it's about our relationship to Creation itself.

The Christian relational witness is what gets us into politics because politics is all about people. It is the Christian relational witness that leads us to value, appreciate, and have concern for Creation, people of every nation, tribe, and tongue. This is where the "issues" list can get contentious but even that is part of the redemptive conversation we need to engage—and lead—as Christ's witnesses in the world today.

Transformational: the presence of an ambassador changes the conversation

Finally, there is the transformational witness of the Christian. Or better said, the transformational power of Christ to which we bear witness. Do you believe Jesus changes everything? If not, what or who is excluded?

Certainly there are individuals, institutions, and situations in which and over which a spirit other than Christ is now reigning. But that does not mean God isn't interested in changing that reality. And the ambassadors He sends to be agents of His transforming presence are you and me.

The grandmother sitting next to me at a ladies luncheon started a conversation, saying, "I attended a really extravagant baby shower for a girl whose mother I know. She's living with the baby's father but they have no intention of marrying. I'm glad she's having the baby but I don't understand why they're not getting married."

I asked, "Why would they or why should they?"

Her expression was somewhat horrified and she responded, "Because it's the *right* thing to do!"

I smiled, affirmingly, and then asked, "What I mean is why would this specific couple get married? What's the value of marriage to them? Tell me about their families."

And with that the light began to dawn. She said, "Both of them have parents who got divorced when they were little kids." She paused and I allowed for a time of silence in which the Spirit could work. "They only know the pain of broken marriage. They don't know how good a marriage can be. They only know the pain of their own experience as kids and maybe they don't want that for their child."

She's right and it illuminates a challenge we face as Christians in a culture where the American church failed to claim marriage as sacred ground. Marriage was conceded to the culture long before the Supreme Court decision in *Obergefell* in 2015 which made same-sex marriage legal in America. Churches in America conceded marriage to cultural redefinition when they did not take a firm stand against no-fault divorce. Church discipline is far too rare and too few know the reality of redeemed marriage.

The Millennial generation, those born between 1980 and 2000 (give or take a few years on either end) is numerically the largest generation in American history. They are also the most racially diverse, the most likely to be religiously unaffiliated, and the most likely to see marriage as unrelated to childbearing or rearing. They are also now all chronologically adults (although many are not mature enough to function as such). And while they will replace retiring Baby Boomers in the workplace, unless something radically changes, they will not replace them in the pews of America's churches. Redeeming relationships with this generation of Americans is an urgent calling. Not to insure the institutional future of churches, but to faithfully live out the Great Commission of the Church in this cultural context.

Q: How do we do that?

A: We tell them our story.

There is no arguing with the power of a changed life. In a culture where personal stories trump everything else, the Christian's testimony of personal transformation—liberation from the power of Sin in life and the penalty of Sin in death—remains the single most effective tool God provides to impact others.

The people around us are asking three basic sets of questions. They are asking questions about identity, belonging, and purpose. As Christians we know all of those questions are answered in Jesus Christ. So, if we have the answers to the questions the people around us are asking, why are we not engaged in the cultural conversations of the day? If we are the ambassadors of the King and the Kingdom that offers people a new restored identity, temporal and eternal belonging, and a mission in this life, then isn't it time to unmute and get God back into the conversation?

Q: How?

A: Well, it starts with listening.

Listen to God and listen to the conversation going on around you in the world that He so loves. What are people talking about in the coffee shop, in the bleachers, at the bar, in the waiting room, at the airport? If your ears are plugged with headphones and your routine is designed to avoid contact with other people, you are most certainly missing the divine appointments God has set for you. Consider this, if you start putting yourself in proximity with sinners, over time you might actually meet someone God is interested in reaching with the redemptive good news of the Gospel.

And, to add to the incentive, there's this: if we're not taking God's viewpoint into the conversation at the bar or in the bleachers, then it is not the culture's fault that God's perspective goes unheard. People can't hear what no one is saying. So, the Christian who was in range, but who does a condemnatory drive-by and shoots off a publican "God, I'm glad I'm not like those heathens" prayer, is responsible for the muting of God in that instance. Yes, I know that's harsh, but it wouldn't sting if it weren't also true.

Most people around us every day do not know what they are doing. Nor do they know why they're doing what they're doing. They are not thinking about what they are thinking about. Their commitments are as fluid as the crowds who hailed Jesus as King on Palm Sunday and called for His crucifixion on Thursday. They do not know who they are because they do not know whose they are. They live to the satisfaction of their basest desires because a vision of heaven has not been set before them. That's where we come in. We are the ambassadors of Jesus Christ. We represent a King and a Kingdom that is and always will be. The gates to it stand open right now and we're in the world to show people the way. If you wondered what on earth you are supposed to be doing today, that, my friend, is it. Time to step up to your Somebody calling.

OTHER INTERESTING READS

Want to know whether or not you're operating out of a Biblical worldview?
https://www.culturefaith.com/worldview-measurement-project/

Faith not impacting other areas of life
http://www.pewforum.org/2016/04/12/religion-in-everyday-life/

Interacting in an echo chamber of agreement: Our siloed society
http://lifewayresearch.com/2016/03/30/religious-liberty-on-decline/

QUESTIONS FOR PERSONAL REFLECTION AND GROUP DISCUSSION

1. This chapter starts with a recollection of words the author's mother spoke into her life as a child. What are some words your mom or other influencer spoke into your life and what are you speaking into the lives of children today?
2. How has God been muted in the culture?
3. How do you feel about being called an ambassador of the Kingdom of Heaven? Do you feel equipped to represent God in the world today? If not, discuss some ways to get equipped.
4. How does your role as an ambassador charged with accurately representing your Sovereign change the way you engage in conversations with others?
5. We call them the days of Noah and the days of Daniel because we know and recognize and celebrate their faithfulness to God in the midst of totally perverse times. How then shall we live in order that years from now the days in which we now live will be remembered as the days of _____ (insert your name)?

CHAPTER 3

Truth Has Consequences and So Do Lies

We live among a dis-integrated people in a disoriented culture. Most people are not integrated in their thinking and, therefore, are not integrated in their living. They can rationalize whatever works for them in the moment because they have no belief in, nor relationship to, anything or anyone who is not malleable. Ethics are situational and everything is negotiable. Everything is fluid including their identity, relationships, and moral behavior.

The culture—characterized by media, entertainment, music, fashion, sports, academia, politics, and religion—is simply the fruit produced in a garden collectively tilled, planted, and cultivated by the people who inhabit a place for a time. So, together as Americans we produce a culture that reflects "us." But we are largely dis-integrated in terms of worldview and that results in a culture that is disoriented, dysfunctional, and producing a lot of rotten fruit.

There was a time when the majority of the people in the culture sought to orient their lives in reference to God as revealed in the Bible, but those days are long gone. American culture today possesses no particular orientation to Truth. Without that anchor, the culture simply drifts, decays, and devolves.

Without a fixed, absolute, external reference point, the finite being attempts the futile quest for meaning within.

Imagine a boy in a small fishing boat not far from the shore. Nothing is biting so he leans back for short nap. He awakes in a chilling fog. He cannot discern anything in any direction. There is no north star, no compass, and no land in view. He has no sense of where he's been, where he's going and even if he did, he's not confident he would know how to get there. Everything for the boy becomes fog. In his case, the fog will lift when the sun rises, but in which direction and how far he drifts between now and then is unknowable. Desperation sets in.

People who are searching for a sense of identity apart from God are like the boy in the fog. Knowing not where they came from, where they're going, why they're here or even if they matter; they seek to define themselves and make something of themselves in a world of fog alongside other blind drifters.

With no cosmological, epistemological, metaphysical, and moral compass, you're lost. And lost is nowhere to live. In order to survive, the mind constructs its own reality. But even those who profess to be living the dream are just living a dream—it is still a mirage and they know it. It disappears as easily as it formed in the imagination. The person's identity is only fixed, albeit momentarily, to the self. That does not work because human beings are woefully insufficient points of integration. As finite creations, we are simply not designed to bear the existential weight.

We have arrived at a time in our culture when people have been told lies for so long they live as if those lies are true. The emergence and propagation of fake news feeds on this culture-wide delusion.

People have been led to believe they are the masters of their own destiny while at the same time being convinced there is nothing beyond the earth-bound mortal life they now live. They have been led to believe they can choose to be whatever they want to be, even if what they want to be is not human at all. Transgender, transspecies, transracial and every other attempt to cast off the reality of how God has made people is part of the delusion. Earlier generations would have seen our current confusion for what it is: nonsense. But we have been following down a path of self-definition for so long that, as a culture, we have few means of calling depravity and foolishness out for what they are.

Truth is that which accords with reality and truth has consequences. So too do lies.

Truth produces people who are integrated and free. Lies produce people who are dis-integrated and in bondage. We will talk later in the book about how to live in the freedom of a fully integrated life, but first, let's confront the context of our disoriented culture which is comprised largely of dis-integrated people.

The dis-integrated reality of people in our culture is evident everywhere. There is culture-wide confusion and disorientation about the most basic questions, including what it means to be human.

Four illustrations show just how dis-integrated people in our culture are from their own humanity. First, we will discuss the confusion between human and animal life in the death of Harambe the gorilla. Second, we'll examine the scourge of pornography in contemporary America. Then we'll turn to the undercover videos that revealed the industry using abortions to traffic in fetal organs. Finally, we will address "Burning Man." These four stories illuminate the depth of confusion in our culture about what it means to be human.

Of man and beast:

In May 2015, a four-year-old child fell into the gorilla habitat at the Cincinnati zoo. The gorilla took notice of the child and dragged the boy by his leg in a way you might expect a 450-pound male silverback gorilla to respond to the sudden introduction of a small curious toy. The crowd panicked and the gorilla responded by taking his new toy into an area with a more obstructed view. The Dangerous Animal Response Team assessed that the child was in imminent mortal danger and, with one shot, killed the gorilla, saving the boy.

That is when the furor erupted, "Why not give preferential treatment to Harambe?" "Why kill the representative of a truly endangered species (aka gorilla) when the other ape in the pen (a.k.a. boy) comes from a species that is clearly not endangered?" The incident sparked global protests, questions about the mother's fitness to parent, and debates about the relative value of life.

Eventually, it was determined the zoo enclosure was not up to code and the Dangerous Animal Response Team (DART) did the right thing in shooting the gorilla to save the four-year-old boy. And just as happened in the media frenzy in the wake of the incident, there was a global conversation about the relative moral value of life. At the heart of the matter is a question of deep worldview significance: why place preferential value on the life of the child?

If you're responding to that question with an answer like, "the child is a person and the gorilla is not," then you're right by God's view but wrong by the view of many intellectuals of our day.

The secular mind sees humans as nothing more than slightly more evolved apes. The mind trained up in evolutionary theory sees every ethical situation as relative. There is no moral difference between the species *Homo sapiens* and its near cousin, the gorilla.

As atheist Richard Dawkins was fond of saying, only "Christian-inspired attitudes" favor humans over other animals species.

So, from a secular worldview, because the gorilla represents an endangered species and the boy represented a non-endangered species, it can certainly be argued that preferential value should have been placed on the life of the gorilla.

The argument is also made that the gorilla was just behaving like a gorilla is expected to behave and the human (a toddler in this case), representing a more evolved species, bears the responsibility of the consequences of his action of entering the pit. The accountability should have befallen the boy, not the gorilla who was simply acting out of his nature.

If you are protesting this as nonsense then you need to know these are the ethics being taught at the nation's leading institutions of higher education. Peter Singer is the chief philosopher behind the animal liberation movement and an ethics professor at Princeton University. His ideas are influencing the thinking of the next generation of America's leaders. In specific response to the reporting on Harambe's death Singer says, "Even sympathetic coverage of Harambe's death referred to him as 'it' or 'the gorilla that' as opposed to 'the gorilla who,' an indication of his lower moral status."[1] To question whether or not an animal has a lower moral status than a person reveals much about the Darwinian effects on American thought.

From a Christian and Biblical worldview, human beings are uniquely created in the image of God (Genesis 1:27) with dominion over everything else in all creation (Genesis 1:26) as stewards of it (Genesis 2:15). Appealing to this argument requires that a person recognize the Bible as the self-revelation of God. Many people do not view the Bible in that way and they do not view human life as possessing any greater value or worth than that of the animals from which, they believe, we evolved.

Worldview matters because our worldview influences how we view ourselves, one another, the world we inhabit, and the society in which we live. A worldview which sees animals and human beings on equal moral footing elevates the one beyond its rightful status and diminishes the glory of the other.

Harambe was a beautiful beast, but a beast nonetheless. The circumstances of his death—on display as a captive example of an animal humanity has nearly driven to extinction—are cause for a moral conversation among the stewards of the earth. But the fact that a gorilla lost his life to preserve the life of a child only causes moral angst for a people who have lost all sense of what it means to be distinctively human.

Dehumanization for our gratification

Once we have successfully dehumanized the person and erased their innate *imago Dei*, we are free to do to them or with them, anything that gratifies our basest desires. We could turn here in two directions: pornography or sex slavery. We will center our conversation here on the nation's sexual obsession and pornography epidemic.

Porn is a national epidemic. This is not the conclusion reached by Christian moralists, but the work of secular scholars. In April of 2016, *Time* did a front-page article titled, "Porn and the threat to virility." The article presented the case that pornography is a national health crisis—effectively making it impossible for a generation of mostly men, but also women, to have healthy intimate relationships. The article states:

> A growing number of young men are convinced that their
> sexual desires have been sabotaged because their brains

were virtually marinated in porn when they were adolescents. Their generation has consumed explicit content in quantities and varieties never before possible, on devices designed to deliver content swiftly and privately, all at an age when their brains were more plastic—more prone to permanent change—than in later life. These young men fell like unwitting guinea pigs in a largely unmonitored decade-long experiment in sexual conditioning.[2]

Pornography is the objectification of a person for sexual gratification. For a long time, the prevailing wisdom of the world was porn provides "consequence free" sexual gratification whenever, however, one wants. It wasn't hurting anybody. Much like the idea that the pill paved the way for the lie that sex could be had "consequence free," the proliferation of pornography has proven devastating to the human heart and mind, marriage, the family, and the dignity of the self and others.

We now know neither porn nor the pill are "consequence free." Porn comes with great consequences and thousands of men and women around the world are reaping the consequence of the lie. We are witnessing what happens when we strip people of their God-given value and sex of God's good design.

In response to the epidemic of readily-accessible pornography, we have seen the same people who hail the sexual revolution now unwittingly questioning its underpinnings. We find it written in an op-ed in the *New York Times*, "It's O.K., Liberal Parents, You Can Freak Out about Porn."[3] It is interesting to note that otherwise liberal parents, those who would support a teen's use of contraception in order to facilitate sexual promiscuity, want limits on pornography. Intrinsically, they know sex is designed *for* something. Boundaries are good and allow for flourishing, healthy relationships.

These parents are reading the research and watching the consequences in real life. But even as they try to draw lines when it comes to hardcore porn and its accessibility for children, they remain unwilling to admit the problem is moral and spiritual. The challenge as a culture is exactly *where* do you draw the lines if you've pulled up the anchor on any moral authority?

Because this is a conversation many Christians have been on the wrong side of for decades, confession and a reorientation to the truth on matters of human dignity and sexuality are essential before entering the conversational fray. But enter we must.

Sexual rights trump human rights

Having made a god of sexual gratification and bifurcating sex from procreation and procreation from marriage, it should be no great surprise Americans have rationalized their way to the extermination of tens of millions of its children through abortion. From 2015 to 2017 the Center for Medical Progress released a series of videos exposing the cavalier manner in which abortion is regarded by providers.

The videos revealed the practice of using the abortion industry to traffic in the organs of prenatal human beings. The criminal justice system failed to see cause for charges because nothing recorded in the videos was found to be illegal. Again, that should give us pause when we consider the moral status of our culture.

There is no question if you watch the videos (which should come with an R rating for graphic violence and inhumane horror) that what you are looking at is a dismembered human baby. And yet, the abortion industry and the entire pro-choice movement deny that very fact. The delusion related to abortion is culture-wide.[4]

Why do so many Americans believe the lie abortion is not murder and the prenatal person is not a person? Because rationalization has powerful mind-altering effects. The related issue for the Christian is the question of medical and technological advances making things possible that are, nonetheless, immoral. We rationalize that because we don't want a baby right now, abortion within a certain window of time is not murder and we also rationalize that when we want a baby, all available medical technology should be brought to bear to make the baby we want when we want it. Similar issues now assert themselves at the other end of life where increasingly people want the option of choosing the manner and time of their own death.

The Bible makes clear that freedom is not to be used as a license to sin. "Everything is permissible but not everything is helpful" (I Corinthians 10:23). Just because we "can" does not mean we "should."

Planned Parenthood dominates the abortion industry. They now have both a hundred-year history and a hundred-year plan. Celebrating the slaughter of more than sixty million American babies since the U.S. Supreme Court ruling in *Roe v. Wade* in 1973, Planned Parenthood now intends for abortion to be the primary American export to the rest of the world. Under the banner of liberty, reduced to sexual freedom, and under the guise of supplying women around the world with the same level of comprehensive healthcare U.S. women have under Obamacare, Planned Parenthood wants to make abortion available to women everywhere. And they want the American taxpayer to fund it.

In 2016 they had their candidate and they succeeded in making their agenda a plank in the platform of the Democratic Party. Hillary Clinton's loss to Donald Trump might have been a blow to the abortion industry but, instead, it was a financial boon.

In the week following the 2016 election when their champion, Hillary Clinton was defeated, Planned Parenthood had a wave of financial contributions unprecedented in its history. Fueled by Cecile Richards's prediction that *Roe v. Wade* would be reversed by a Supreme Court nominated by Trump, people gave historic amounts of money to an organization committed to the extermination of the next generation of Americans. Think about that. Does that make any sense?

Well, it makes sense if you believe, along with Hillary Clinton, a person has no constitutional rights until they are outside the womb. That's what she said on *Meet the Press* during the 2016 campaign cycle. "The unborn person doesn't have constitutional rights."[5] Now, let's look at that sentence. She concedes that what is in the womb is, in fact, an unborn person. She then declares that unborn person lacks constitutional rights. How is that a morally consistent evaluation of personhood? It's not, of course, which is the point. The goal is not consistency, the presentation of an integrated view of reality, or a life aligned with any moral reference point outside of the self. The goal is to say and do whatever is relatively expedient to rationalize my own self-interested priorities. That sentence may describe the current cultural thinking on abortion and a myriad of other issues, but it is the antithesis of the mind of Christ (Philippians 2).

The idea we can be whatever we want to be obliterates the theological claim that we are created intentionally by God and we are already fully known. Anyone who holds to a position allowing for abortion under anything but the strictest conditions does not believe God is the one knitting babies together in a mother's womb. Or, if they do, then they think we know better than God. Either way, the status of our culture's collective moral conscience is found to be corrupt.

Abortion is the leading cause of death in America and has been for decades. More Americans die as a result of the intentional termination of their life by their own mother than by any other cause. That should come as a trauma to our conscience, but for many it's quite the opposite. The argument is now made that pro-life "propaganda" is a threat to the psyche of a woman seeking an abortion and has been banned by courts in Europe and Canada. Anti-abortion advocates face often violent opposition on U.S. college campuses even when they are making their pro-life arguments in "free speech zones."

The idea underlying abortion is the myth of autonomy or the total sovereignty of the self. The assertion of individual autonomy, it should be noted, is only argued on behalf of the women seeking to control a situation which is clearly beyond her control. Consider the hypocrisy of asserting that a woman has full sovereignty over her own body and the right to assert nihilistic control over the life another, smaller, weaker, person. How can the one have absolute rights and the other absolutely none? If you were looking for an example of dis-integrated thinking, there it is.

Idolization of identity

Beyond the highly charged political debates surrounding abortion, there is yet a deeper identity confusion in our culture. We're talking of course about the sexual orientation and gender identity (SOGI) revolution. What used to be known as gay and lesbian concerns grew into an alphabet long list that currently includes LGBTTQQIAAP (lesbian, gay, bisexual, transgender, transsexual, queer, questioning, intersex, asexual, ally, pansexual). You would have to Google "What is the full acronym for LGBT" to get an up-to-date acronym, but at some point the foolishness of that became apparent to the advocates themselves and a new comprehensive moniker was chosen: SOGI. That language has been fully adopted by the federal government, media, entertainment industry, institutions of higher education, and downstream of these cultural influencers into the common vernacular of our nation.

Although it's confusing, if we listen carefully and read closely, there are signs of the residue of the unchanging Truth even in what are intended to be efforts at advocacy for the sexual and moral revolution. For example, in 2016 the *Atlanta Journal Constitution* essay contest resulted in the publication of a highly emotional piece titled, "Emma Is a Boy."[6] The essay chronicles the experience of a mother (no mention is made of a father) as she embraces the reality that her twelve-year-old daughter perceives herself to be a boy.

Here's the critical reference point: when the mother is crying out to God about the issue, God responds, "love her." It happens three times according to the essay. God says, "Love her, love her, love her." Love *her*. So, contrary to the article's title, contrary to the child's gender confusion, and contrary to the mother's willingness to accommodate the confusion, from God's perspective, Emma is a *her*, a girl.

Evidence of the gender confusion of contemporary America is not difficult to find. New York City lists thirty-one different gender identities expressly protected by its anti-discrimination laws. Teachers are encouraged to refrain from calling their students "boys" and "girls" because it unduly categorizes individuals. In 2014, users of Facebook were offered a third option in terms of gender identity and that third option opened a portal into fifty-eight choices. By 2017 that list had grown to seventy-one. Having expanded the definition of marriage beyond one man and one woman, Americans are exploring a myriad of marriage models.

Q: But that kind of thinking is only supported by the far left fringe, right?

A: Wrong. In fact, if you think that's fringe thinking, you're considered the fringe thinker.

Those who continue to hold that marriage should be exclusively between one man and one woman—who were born genetically and anatomically as male and female—are considered the "extreme fringe" of cultural conversations. If you agree marriage is created, ordered, and blessed by God to be uniquely between one man and one woman in monogamy until death do they part, you have adopted a moral position expressly contrary to the prevailing opinion of the culture. But that does not make you wrong and you are not alone. You may be standing for a season on culture's perceived "wrong side of history" but you are standing there with the holy God.

Having begun the journey down the path of gender confusion, where does it end?

What if a person does not feel like a person at all. Instead, they feel like an animal, or a mythical creature? This actually happened when a man had his nose and ears removed in pursuit of transforming himself.

The celebration of sexual and gender confusion is now a part of mainstream journalism. *Time* magazine ran a feature length story about a transgendered man, who although he was no longer a woman, had always wanted to give birth. So with the help of medical professionals, he gave birth and nursed a child. This was celebrated as "remaking the American family." It sounds outlandish, but that is the point. When there is no absolute standard against which to test our ideas, there is no moral compass. How and where do we then draw the lines? The answer is "anywhere we so choose."

Sexual and gender confusion epitomize how dis-integrated and disoriented we have become as a culture. Having muted God, we have only our own thoughts and the ideas of other people to feed our imagination. Identity politics and self-definition are the order of the day as American idols rise and fall in seemingly endless cycles of celebrity based on nothing more than making a name for oneself.

Devoid of God's perspective, empty people will seek to fill in the blanks of their lives with whatever or whomever is at hand. People are seeking to hold it all together themselves, when, in fact, they were never meant to be their own point of integration. And although we have been trying since the Beginning to come up with a viable alternative to God as the center, Jesus alone is sufficient to that task.

Seeking what only God can provide

There is an annual festival, which takes place in Nevada every summer. It's called Burning Man. If you have not heard of it, the festival has been in existence for over thirty years. Attendance in 2016 was seventy thousand people, making the temporary settlement the state's third largest city for the week. It is popular among tech moguls and celebrities. There are parties and bands and extensive art installations. The purpose is whatever you want it to be. Self-discovery, pleasure, and fulfillment draw thousands every year.

What is most interesting is what's at the center of the temporary metropolis and culmination of the event: an edifice of a man. Then, at the end of the week, all of it burns. People do not just trek to the middle of the desert for a good party. They are searching for something—for inspiration, freedom, belonging. They want something life changing.

Burning Man encapsulates what is written on our hearts. We desire significance and meaning—we seek for truth. But like Burning Man displays, a search that ends outside God is finally futile. We end up trekking into the desert to worship an idol made in our own image that is consumed in our attempt to worship that which cannot bear the weight of it. Literally a "burning man" collapsing in on itself.

That visage bears physical witness to the spiritual reality that secular humanism has proven insufficient as a moral philosophy by which to orient an individual life let alone a culture. Postmodernism is an even worse failure. Instead of developing well-oriented, healthy, integrated people, these philosophies have distorted the truth, bred confusion, and laid waste to the very foundation of the people who make the culture. Abortion, eugenics, assisted suicide, and welfare dependency are all evidences of the utilitarian or pragmatic nature of self-interested secular humanism.

The Christian may have adapted to the environment in order to survive, but the truth is the Christian worldview is radically opposed to much of what the culture asserts about what it means to be human.

The Christian worldview recognizes that people are image bearers of the living God and in His Creative wisdom, God made them explicitly male and female. We didn't come up with the idea of a man and woman being joined together in holy matrimony to become one flesh. That's God's idea and it's a reflection of the eternal relationship He has with the Church as the Bride of Christ. When we mess with gender, sex, and marriage we're messing with realities that belong to the purview of God. Again it comes down to me or Thee.

The Christian worldview also recognizes that God is sovereign over human life from conception to natural death—and to the life beyond death. For human beings to take life into their own hands, to act as if anyone but God could be sovereign over the life of another image bearer through abortion, human enslavement, or assisted suicide is pure idolatry.

You may be saying to yourself, "Don't Americans already know that?" No, they don't, but you're just the person to tell them.

There was a time when the Christian worldview could be assumed among most Americans. That day is long gone. The foundations began to be undermined in mainline Christianity in the very early twentieth century, and since the mid-1960s secular moral revolutionaries have been shaping the American mind through all levels of education, the courts, the entertainment industry, and now through social media. Of particular destructive influence have been the organized advocacy of sexual revolutionaries and the willing participation in that movement by mainline Protestant denominations.

The challenge of our times is this: if the self is the ultimate arbiter of truth and truth is relative, then who are we to say anything is wrong with any of this? But, we've been here before, in the days the Bible calls the days of the Judges. And we also know the remedy: Gospel revival.

If you want to see just how bad it can get when a culture pulls up the anchor of God's unchanging Word and begins to chart its own self-determined course, read the book of Judges. By the time we arrive at chapter nineteen it is fair to say all hell has broken loose in the lives of the people. There is no evil they will not do and there is no restraint.

No, we're not there yet. But the path of lies down which we are collectively trekking has consequences. Just as Truth has consequences, so do lies.

QUESTIONS FOR PERSONAL REFLECTION AND GROUP DISCUSSION

1. Have you ever been lost—in a city or in a fog or at sea? How did you find your way back to a point of reference you recognized or did you wait to be found?
2. Can you describe or point to examples of dis-integrated people and disoriented culture?
3. How can the Good News compete in the marketplace of ideas of fake news, fifteen minute news cycles, and instantaneous social media? Discuss several possibilities.
4. How might you respond to families dealing with one of the concerns listed in this chapter?
   a. People who treat pets or animals as if they are people
   b. Pornography and other sexuality issues like sexual abuse, violence, and human trafficking
   c. Abortion and other life-related issues like the so-called "right to die"

CHAPTER 4

I Know Something's Wrong, but What's Right?

We read a headline that breaks our heart or see an image that turns our stomach and we ask, "What's wrong with us?" We see the evidence of brokenness all around us. We know the casualties and costs of war in the world, in the workplace, in our homes and in our hearts. We all know something is wrong. We know *this* is not the way it is supposed to be.

We imagine there must have been better times by some measures, but we also know that even in those "good old days" things were only relatively good and for relatively few. If we think about it long enough we come to the conclusion the last time things were actually good, objectively good, was in the days prior to the Fall. But we live so far from Eden it is hard to even imagine what objective goodness looked like, let alone felt like.

What was it like to live in perfect harmony with God, the self, the other, and Creation?

What was it like to walk with God and talk with Him, unashamed?

What was it like to breathe air saturated with oxygen and devoid of pollution?

What was it like to love in an atmosphere of total trust, free of suspicion?

What was it like to know fully and be fully known with no self-doubt, guilt, or shame?

What was it like to know only good and know no evil?

In a word: perfect.

In a phrase: heaven on earth.

In an image: paradise ...

Lost.

Since the Fall, humanity has been playing what can be described as a game of Hide n' Seek. In Genesis 3 we learn Adam and Eve followed Sin's domino effect all the way down the path of destruction. The Bible tells us "their eyes were opened and they were ashamed." And then the text reads (emphasis added),

> Then the man and his wife heard the sound of the LORD God as he was walking in the garden in the cool of the day, and *they hid from the LORD God* among the trees of the garden.
>
> But the LORD God called to the man, "Where are you?" (Genesis 3:7–9)

In Hide 'n Seek parlance God says to Adam and Eve, "Come out, come out, wherever you are." They essentially respond, "We're hiding and you're it!"

From that fateful day to this, we've never stopped hiding and God in His grace has never stopped seeking

I remember one particular game of Hide 'n Seek when I was a child. My hiding place was superb—I would be sure to win. The seeker would never think to look where I hid. I would never be found! That, in fact turned out to be true. All the other kids were found, eventually the seeker gave up and they all moved on to a game of Kick the Can in the cul-de-sac on Roxmere Road.

I don't remember how long I waited to be found, but at some point I peeked out and realized what happened. I was mad and my feelings were hurt. How could they just quit? The game was Hide 'n *Seek*—not hide and wander off when you get tired of looking. How could the seeker have just given up on finding me?

On a cosmic level, this never happens. No matter where we hide—even to the depths—and no matter how long we hide, God never gives up seeking us. Assurance of that fact comes in Psalm 139:7–10:

> Where shall I go from your Spirit?
> Or where shall I flee from your presence?
> If I ascend to heaven, you are there!
> If I make my bed in Sheol, you are there!
> If I take the wings of the morning
> and dwell in the uttermost parts of the sea,
> even there your hand shall lead me,
> and your right hand shall hold me.

And Jesus assures us as well when He confirms He came to "seek and to save the lost" (Luke 19:10).

We may graduate from the childhood version of Hide 'n Seek but until we allow ourselves to be found by the Savior, we never stop trying to hide from God.

- From our hidden agendas to our secret dalliances
- From the fears and doubts we keep tucked away to the New Age practices we participate in on the side
- From the things we keep hidden from friends to the desires we keep secret from our spouses
- From the assets we try to hide as we determine our tithe to the weak human frailties we try to hide in community with one another

Worse yet, we hide our own hiding from ourselves. We cry out, "Why, oh why, O God, do you hide from me? Why are You so far from me?" All the while failing to see it is not God who is hiding, but ourselves.

The truth is nothing is hidden from God. God sees it all, hears it all, reads it all, and knows it all. There is no firewall that keeps God out. The Psalmist affirms there is nowhere on earth we can flee from God—wherever we may go, God is present.

Games of Hide 'n Seek are not new. The Bible is replete with examples:

- Adam and Eve tried to hide their sin from God and the cost was expulsion from the Garden of Eden
- Achan tried to hide the forbidden spoils of Jericho's destruction from Joshua and the consequence was his death
- Saul tried to hide the equally forbidden spoils of the destruction of the Amalekites and God rejected Saul as king, anointing David
- Jonah tried to avoid God's call by hiding on a ship and when God found him he had to spend three days in the belly of a whale

- Ananias and Sapphira tried to hide the benefit of their financial blessing from the early church and when their sin was found out they both died

Playing Hide 'n Seek with God is a dangerous game!

But the good news remains: the seeking Savior of the lost is the very nature of Christ.

What's wrong with us and the world is we're still hiding from God. *What's right* is a world where we allow ourselves to be found and allow God to restore us to right relationship with Him, ourselves, one another, and the Creation He made for us to manage.

If you're still hiding, this invitation is for you today: Jesus Christ came to seek and save the lost. He is the one who seeks and he will not rest until we are found. Aren't you ready to be found?

When I was young I misunderstood the announcement of grace spoken at the end of the game. I heard (and repeated) "Ollie, Ollie oxen free!" when in fact the declaration rings, "All in, all in, all in free!"

That is mercy and grace. In Jesus Christ you are invited to come out of hiding, "all in, all in, all in free." The God of all mercy and grace is seeking to save you. He wants to welcome you with love, graft you into a great family of faith, and become your new hiding place—your shelter, your protection, your sure defense, and your eternal home.

Aren't you tired of hiding? Haven't you been on the lamb long enough? Isn't it time to come out of hiding, rely on the Lamb of God who takes away the sins of the world, and live in the light of God's love? If you've never done so, let today be the day you respond to the Lord who calls out, "Come out, come out, wherever you are!" And realize God, in His grace, is calling, "All in, all in, all in free!"

Facing the reality of a world in hiding from God

From the Garden of Eden we fast forward many millennia and find ourselves right where God told us we would be: with the knowledge of good and evil, but without the wisdom to handle the difference. We range about looking for fixed reference points that continue to elude us. All is in flux and we find all that uncertainty is not, in fact, freedom. Our minds wander and find all kinds of things on which to set.

The mind is a miraculous thing. According to God *the mind can be set*, "those who live according to the flesh *set their minds* on the things of the flesh, but those who live according to the Spirit *set their minds* on the things of the Spirit. For to *set the mind* on the flesh is death, but to *set the mind* on the Spirit is life and peace" (Romans 8:5–6). And according to God, *the mind can be reset*, "Do not be conformed to this world, but be transformed by the *renewal of your mind*, that by testing you may discern what is the will of God, what is good and acceptable and perfect" (Romans 12:2; emphasis added).

An individual can be out of their right mind and can be restored to a right mind by Jesus Christ (Luke 8:35; Acts 26:24). A person's mind can be debased (Romans 1:28), hostile to God and alienated from Him (Colossians 1:21). Our minds can be hardened, sensuous (Colossians 2:18), depraved (I Timothy 6:5), corrupted (II Timothy 2:8), defiled (Titus 1:15), duplicitous (James 1:8), foolish, and darkened (Romans 1:21; Ephesians 4:18). But praise be to God, our minds can also be changed, renewed, restored, reset, revived, sobered, enlightened, conformed to the very mind of Christ, unified, wise, and sincere.

Contrary to the opinion of some, people of faith are not unthinking sycophants mindlessly parroting mythical nonsense. The Christian faith is a thinking faith. The Great Commandment includes the love of God with all the mind. Even in the context of prayer and praise and singing, the Christian is mindful (1 Corinthians 14:15).

God reveals that the process of sanctification includes the conformation of the mind of the believer to the very mind of Christ. God's

Word leads us "think about these things," (Philippians 4:8) and to "set our minds" on certain things and not on others (Colossians 3:2). And Jesus tells us even a disciple can become mindless. Remember his rebuke of Peter in Mark 8:33? "Get behind me, Satan! For you are not setting your mind on the things of God, but on the things of man."

Just as Jesus's own family thought he was "out of his mind" at one point (Mark 3:21), the world often sees Christians as lunatics. We must hold fast to the truth that the mind of Christ is perfectly aligned with the heart of God no matter what the shifting mind of the world may say.

Q: Am I out of my mind?

A: Yes, because I am seeking to have the mind of Christ. And God's thoughts are not my thoughts and His ways are not my ways. I have to be out of mind and into His if I want to be an authentic representative of His will in the world.

The challenge for the Christian is to see the world from this "in the world but not of it" dual perspective in order to be able to speak authentically for Christ with relevance to the realities people are facing. If I know the mind of Christ, but I'm out of touch with the matters of the day, I cannot bring His mind to bear on reality in a way that helps others. So, what's on the mind of the world and how is the worldly mind set?

The mindset of the world today

Remember postmodernism? We don't often hear the term used because it's now simply the water we're swimming in. Postmodernism is a philosophy as well as a movement. It denies objective reality and absolute truth. Postmodern thinkers reject religion because truth claims, ideologies, and grand narratives are considered suspect. Which means they think it's just all made up—examples of some system of social construction in the past designed by one group to somehow control or dominate or subjugate another. Why? Because to the post-modern way of thinking, truth and knowledge are produced. Yes, produced. Knowledge and truth are seen as products of particular historical, political, and social systems. Everything is contextual. All ethics are situational. Morality is relative. Reality is self-referential and the individual's life is simultaneously devoid of any ultimate meaning and held out as ultimately meaningful.

Welcome to postmodernity where there's no objective there there (no, that's not a typo).

Imagine you are a turtle or maybe a dolphin in the Red Sea. You know the difference between air and water. You've been above the surface and you know how to breathe there. You also know no fish with whom you swim can survive in that environment. But it's not a problem because there's always water where they are. There's always water *there*, in every direction. Well, until that one time when there was not.

When the water stood up like walls to allow the Israelites to pass through on dry land and then crushed back down upon their Egyptian pursuers, what was going on with the fish? How could the fish have possibly known not to swim *there*? Where's *there* if you're a fish? Water is water, unless it's suddenly air. Christians are like the dolphins or the turtles of the Red Sea. We are trying to figure out how to communicate a word of warning to the culture not to go *there*. And yet, *there* they go.

Once I acknowledged the reality of postmodernity as the cultural water we're swimming in, I was no longer surprised at the irrational, dis-integrated, illogical decisions people make. If truth is a product of a context and the context changes, then the truth changes. Perfectly reasonable, right? Yes, if you've been raised in the postmodern waters of late twentieth- and early twenty-first-century America. Simultaneously espousing one thing and doing another or simultaneously espousing two diametrically opposed ideas as equally true is not irrational to the postmodern mind.

Read that again and let it sink in: *Simultaneously espousing one thing and doing another or simultaneously espousing two diametrically opposed ideas as equally true is not irrational to the postmodern mind.*

The theory of "cognitive dissonance" was first developed by Dr. Leon Festinger in the 1950s as he was studying the human striving for internal consistency. We have described that here as integration and the reality of dis-integration with which many in our culture are living. When inconsistency (dissonance) is experienced, individuals tend to become psychologically uncomfortable because it's cognitively painful to hold two opposing beliefs at the same time. In the past, people have chosen to adapt in order to bring beliefs into alignment with reality. Christians would call this the conforming of the life to Christ. But increasingly postmoderns are trying to live with the mental stress of holding two or more contradictory beliefs, ideas, or values at the same time. Living with cognitive dissonance over a prolonged period of time may have deleterious effects on the individual and community but from a selfie culture perspective, that's a problem for someone else to deal with.

To the Christ-minded person, cognitive dissonance is nothing more than irrationality. And again, it's not a new problem.

This Alice in Wonderland reality offers up combinations and fusions of all kinds of formerly distinct concepts. Once good is evil and evil good, combining concepts like "gay Christian" or "transgender male mother" or "atheist pastor" becomes rational. We also arrive at the place where those demanding absolute liberty for themselves see no hypocrisy in demanding total capitulation by others to their self-referential truth claims. The postmodern sees no conflict in arguing on the one hand for the immutability of the same-sex attracted person and the right of the individual to choose gender reassignment (now known as gender confirmation) surgery. And then expect that surgery and all necessary supports to be paid for by others.

Understanding the context of postmodernity, we are less surprised at the contradictory findings of surveys revealing that many of the views held by a majority of Americans are heretical by historical Christian standards. The postmodern mind is able to hold many contradictory truths as simultaneously true. So, the postmodern is picking and choosing the parts and pieces they like and aggregating their own synchronized individualized religious practices. They may well still call it Christianity, until they decide to call it something else.

To the postmodern mind, nothing is fixed, including the meaning of words. The postmodern mind does not acknowledge anyone has the right to lay permanent claim to the meaning of anything. It's all flexible. What it meant when it meant what you think it meant was a former context. Now it means something else. Which means we have to define everything. "What do you mean by everything?" you ask. Good question!

I attended two workshops at an LGBT advocacy conference at a mainline liberal church in Chicago. The first was on the non-linear sexual identity and the second on non-binary relationships.[1]

After introductions around the semicircle of eight participants, the self-described bisexual ordained minister shared a list of definitions to provide a working lexicon for attendees.

Bisexuality was defined as attraction to people of one's own gender and people of other genders. Pansexual and polysexual were introduced as terms related to bisexuality as "both terms describe people whose attractions move beyond a single gender." By contrast we were told, "gay, lesbian, and straight" people are described as "monosexual" because they are attracted to exclusively one gender. The workshop leader added that "monosexuals are considered privileged by bisexual people."

Polyamory was defined as "consensual non-monogamous," or "the practice, desire, or acceptance of intimate relationships that are not exclusive with respect to other intimate relationships, with the knowledge and consent of all involved." We were then informed that a person might be bisexual monogamous or bisexual polyamorous. Queer was then added as "an umbrella term for those whose sexual and/or gender fall outside of heterosexuality and cisgender."

Cisgender, you ask? So did I. I was told we would be getting to that. But first she defined "transgender as a gender identity that does not align with the sex assigned to a person at birth," offering three related terms:

- Gender queer (the bisexuality of gender—which can be fluid)
- Cisgender—a person's gender identity is coherent with the sex they were assigned at birth
- Agender—a person who does not identify with a specific gender

When a question about agender was raised, the workshop participant who identified as an asexual-polyamorous-trans-woman, further explained that "a non-binary person rejects the distinct difference between male and female. They don't think of it as a linear scale but as a galaxy of orbits that are ever changing."

A galaxy of orbits was a very good description.

The second workshop was designed as a splainer of gender identity and sexual orientation concerns to old fashioned cisgender people like me.

A candidate for ministry who has since been ordained in a mainline denomination led the workshop. Born anatomically female, this individual identified as a trans-man and was married to a woman. "He" said, "there is a plurality of gender expression, but self-named gender identity is where the power is."

Self-named gender identity is where the power is. Think about that statement. Contrast this with what Paul says about emptying the cross of its power, or being ashamed of the Gospel, which is the power of salvation to those who believe.

Back to the workshop: we were then invited to introduce ourselves with a preferred pronoun and any other gender or sexual orientation identifiers we felt would help the group honor us. When it came around to me I introduced myself as a cis-female who prefers female pronouns. It sounded strange when I said it then and it still sounds strange today.

Workshops participants were expected to follow a list of stated "covenants," including:

- "Valuing people in the nuances of their experience which can be wildly infinite vs. limiting people to clearly delineated definitions or boxes,"
- "Being hospitable by inviting questions but not lurid, invasive or inappropriate,"
- "Being vulnerable by taking risks while maintaining self-care, knowing your own comfortable limits."

We were then introduced to two graphics that would provide the basis of conversation. Again, remember, we're talking about how terms are defined and how those terms are then used to redefine our perception of reality.

The first image is "a gender binary," straight-line thinking about a subject that was argued is no longer seen as this straightforward. The second image is the continuum of gender-fluid options now understood as normal.

The first diagram describes what was labeled in the workshop as "sexist and sexually repressed system designed to control people and put them in boxes." The workshop presenter contended it was past time to do away with the straight line thinking and replace it with thinking along a spectrum.

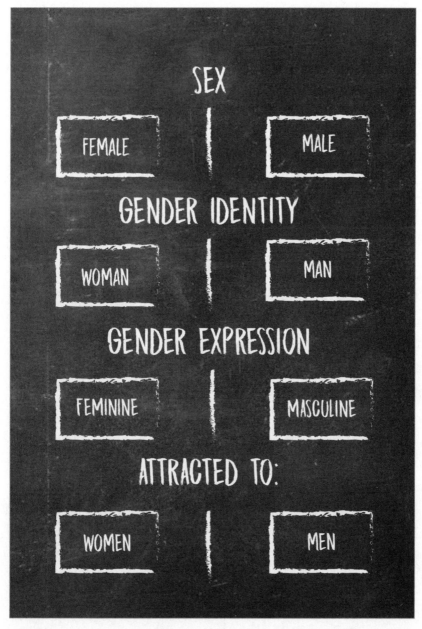

Content of slide shown at Covenant Network of Presbyterians "Marriage Matters" workshop, 2013. *Graphic designer: Mary Scarlett Greenway*

Then the time came for the lexicon, the all-important defining of terms.

Noting "even biological sex is not as fixed as you might have thought," and "the choice made at birth by doctors and parents may or may not align with the person down the continuum over time." Gender fluidity was introduced as a term to describe a person who fluctuates over time or even day-to-day on the gender expression spectrum. And then came the conversation about use of the pronoun *they*.

Q: Can we use "they" to describe an individual?

A: Yes, and it is being used with increasing frequency by the courts and educators.

Check out this Q&A on a website designed to promote gender nonconformity (Emphasis added):

> My fifth grade teacher always told me using "they" as a singular pronoun was grammatically incorrect. Is my fifth grade teacher wrong about that?
>
> While I'm sure your fifth grade teacher meant well when they were teaching you the rules about pronouns, *the rules you learned in fifth grade are most likely outdated by now.* In fact, the 200 linguists at the American Dialect Society *declared the singular "they" the 2015 word of the year.* Merriam-Webster and the Oxford dictionary both also include the singular "they."[2]
>
> Whether your fifth grade teacher likes it or not, "they" is now a recognized and *grammatically correct* singular pronoun.
>
> Also, I don't know the gender identity of your fifth grade teacher, which is why I used "they," rather than "he or she." Not only is "they" a more streamlined option, "they" also allows room for the possibility that your fifth grade teacher didn't identify as a man or a woman at all!

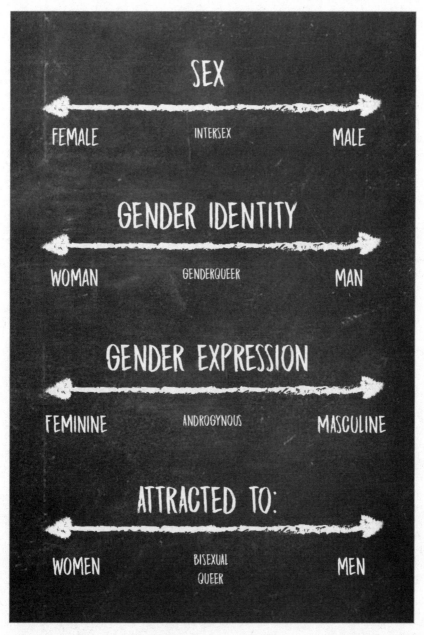

Content of slide shown at Covenant Network of Presbyterians "Marriage Matters" workshop, 2013. *Graphic designer: Mary Scarlett Greenway*

Maybe they were genderqueer. Maybe they were nonbi-
nary. I don't know their gender, so I'm not going to arti-
ficially limit your fifth grade teacher's gender identity to
one of two options. It's a more inclusive, fabulous way to
go about it.[3]

Those of us who seek to engage in meaningful conversation now
need a lexicon.

In both workshops, after the defining of terms, the remainder of
the time was devoted to the telling of stories. And that's the way into
the conversation for you and me. We have a story to tell as well and
the postmodern mind loves a good story especially when it's got show
and tell.

Your personal story is undeniable and people want to hear your
story. Where God appears in your story, the more personal you
can make it, the better. God is not an idea, God is a real person.
Avoid direct reference to the Bible and no reference to "my church
teaches" because although those are authorities for you they are
not accepted as authoritative to others. Stick with statements that
begin with:

- In my experience ...
- I have come to see ...
- My study has led me to believe ...

Talk about the dark valleys, the times of doubt, the wounds and
wanderings. Your conversation partners know pain and they know
loneliness. But God has wired them the same way He wired you and
me—with a very deep desire for a restored relationship with Him. If
you can tell your story and aren't afraid to show the path through the
wilderness you wandered, you just may find they'll walk with you
long enough to find the Way themselves.

If you're thinking right now, "I don't have a story," that's simply not true. If it helps, grab a piece of paper and draw your life on a timeline from conception to the present. Fill in the highs and lows and then fill in all the in-betweens. Start with the circumstances of your conception. Were your parents married, unmarried, are you the product of IVF or rape? Do you know who your father is? What were the circumstances of your birth? Were you a preemie or adopted or born with a condition? Have you survived cancer? Are you living with chronic pain or disability? Were you a standout athlete? Did you win the lottery? Are you divorced, widowed, never married and wishing you were? Are you childless but wish you weren't? Have you walked with someone you love to the end of the valley of death and then come back through the grief to life redefined? Were you a prodigal? Do you have a history (directly or indirectly) of addiction? Did someone you love take their own life? Have you been homeless, hungry, or unable to pay the bills? Have you been to war or suffered the post-traumatic stress of it with someone you love? Is your child not like all the other kids? Do you have an eating disorder? Were you a victim of assault or abuse? Have you ever been to jail? *You have a story.*

I asked Andrea Casteel Smith for permission to tell her story and she agreed. She tells the whole story in *Scarred Beautiful*, but to summarize: By all accounts, Andrea had it all. Family, financial security, faith community, beauty, friends—until the night she was arrested in her own driveway for driving under the influence. She'd only driven a few blocks. She'd only had a few drinks, but she bore the full weight of the penalty of her sin including spending a month in the county jail. She was broken at every level of her being and the lowest point came when her physical scars, the result of skin grafts when she was an infant, were exposed in multiple strip searches with male guards looking on. Andrea tells her story of redemption with a piercing authenticity that cuts through skepticism. You cannot read her story and deny the reality of the God who was there, the God who spoke, the God who healed, the God who redeemed, and the God who has now given her a new purpose in helping other scarred beautiful people tell their stories as well.[4]

If you are a redeemed sinner, you have a story. And that story is the undeniable truth of the Gospel through which God desires to reach into the heart of another.

You have a story and it's eternal. Every person you ever meet on every day of every year is a person with an eternal story. Your story has the power to influence another person's perspective on life and themselves and God and eternity. That, my friend, is a Gospel calling!

I have a friend whose upbringing from the outside appeared idyllic. Two well-educated upwardly mobile parents with good jobs, nice neighborhood, excellent schools. But his parents were cultural Catholics and his mother constantly reminded him that had it not been for the Church making her feel forced to have him, she would have never married his dad and her life would be so much different. She has told him more than once that he ruined her life. "She would have been" any number of things, if not for him. He was an accident and she had only married his father because she was pregnant. She hadn't really wanted kids so he would only ever be an only child. Just thinking about it breaks my heart.

But God had a plan for my friend from before the foundations of the earth. God was working out that plan when He was knitting my friend together in his mother's womb. Discovering God's redeeming love in Jesus Christ has given my friend a new identity and sense of himself. As John 1:12–13 promises, as one who has received Christ, and believed in His name, my friend has become a child of God—born not of human decision or a human's will, but born of God. He is not a mistake, but a chosen child born on purpose and for a purpose. He is no longer an only child but one son among billions of brothers and sisters in the household of God. You have a story and its personal.

What Americans are missing is the reality that God is a person—and not just any person. God's nature as holy and sovereign and merciful actually means something—and that something is not up for endless personal interpretation and reinterpretation as the winds of time and circumstance blow.

God alone has the right and the privilege of defining what is good and beautiful and true. Those transcendent values are the only legitimate basis for personal and public morality. But how do you help people see a cosmology when they've come to believe they are the captains of their own destiny? You tell them a story.

Having established authenticity through the sharing of our story and hearing theirs, we make use of the stories of others as well.

The apostle Paul has a story that is not only worth knowing, it's worth repeating. You can use any of the second half of the book of Acts to tell Paul's story or you can use a letter like Philippians. I like to use the book of Philippians because it is short, personal, and rich. The theme of the book is the mind of Christ. And we want to be cultivating the mind of Christ in the matters of the day so it's an essential book for us to know. In it Paul not only testifies to the mind in Christ but demonstrates what a life governed by the mind of Christ looks like. He then calls us to have the mind of Christ as well.

"What's on your mind?" is an easy conversation starter no matter who you're with. It's a wide open door that provides others the opportunity to initiate a subject or volley back to you. "I've been thinking about what God must think about everything going on today. What do you think God thinks about … " and you fill in the blank.

Most people will not have given God much conscious thought. Most will not have considered God's perspective on the issue and many will honestly admit they have no idea what He might think. You, on the other hand, have a mind full of mindful thoughts on the matter! You have been thinking about what you're thinking about. You have been intentionally setting your mind on the things that are above. You have sought God's perspective and the mind of Christ on the matters of the day. You are ready for this!

We know from the Bible what God declares to be good. We also know what He declares to be sin. We know what breaks the heart of God and we know what delights Him. All we have to do now is tell the story.

QUESTIONS FOR PERSONAL REFLECTION AND GROUP DISCUSSION

1. What do you think it was like to walk with God in the perfection of Creation before the Fall?
2. What types of Hide n' Seek have you played with God over the course of your life?
3. Are you still hiding? If so, are you ready to allow yourself to be found? To respond to the Seeking God's "all in, all in, all in free" offer of grace? If not, what stands in your way?
4. How does the description of the nonsensical postmodern mindset help you make sense of the world?
5. What words, images, and concepts have been redefined and need to be returned to what they really mean before we can communicate effectively with the culture?
6. What's your story? (Go back and review page 81 and then write your story.)

CHAPTER 5

The Necessity of Restoring the Word of God to Its Rightful Place

During the Protestant Reformation, five hundred years ago, a saying developed that when translated to English reads, "Reformed and always being reformed, according to the Word of God." By that the Reformers were declaring the Church is a living, dynamic body that continually changes. But they were clear those changes had parameters: notably, the Word of God. In the past hundred years in mainline denominations, the criterion of "according to the Word of God" has been dropped, creating reformations according to the ever-changing preferences of prevailing opinion.

When humanity becomes the standard of judgment, it is not only the Church that suffers, but the world. The Church has a rightful calling and it is not the temporal self-fulfillment nor sexual liberation of those who would see themselves as members of it. The Church is the Bride and the Body of Christ. She is not "ours" so much as she is His. God calls together and sends forth the Church to be a living demonstration of the Gospel of Jesus Christ so others might come to know Him and be saved. Everything else—yes, everything else, is secondary.

Consider this:

All human beings are formed by God.

All are deformed by Sin.

Some become informed by the Word of God.

Some of those are transformed by the renewing of their minds, and

Some of them are conformed to the image of God's Son, Jesus, by

the reforming power of the Holy Spirit.

Some, but not all.

Between the initial comprehensive *all* and the final *some* lies the mission field.

Reformation, individual and cultural, requires the admission that we are deformed and transformation comes not only through information but through conformation to the Word of God.

The Scriptures are formative, informative, restorative, and can be transformative. But we have to make rightful use of them in order for their power to be realized. As the Bible says, we must be doers of the Word and not hearers only. But what does that mean?

The interpretation of the Bible is a matter of seemingly endless debate. But it comes down to this: either God has spoken or He has not. If God has spoken, then what God says matters more than anything we feel, imagine or desire. If God is not real and has not spoken then a very great lie has been perpetrated upon us all.

Accepting that God is real and He has spoken puts us in a reciprocal relationship with Him. Accepting the Bible as the inspired, inerrant Word of God requires us to respond. That response is in the context of a relationship with God in which we grow in our understanding and ability to apply what God has said. Desiring to glorify Him and cause God joy becomes our life's pursuit and our heart's desire.

Like all relationships, this one requires mutual understanding. However, while God fully understands us, we do not fully understand God. The Bible is God's gift of revelation but the Bible admits that a person approaching the Bible with a natural mind only will be unable to understand much of what God says therein. By grace, God enables us by His own Spirit through valid hermeneutics to understand and know Him through the Scriptures. That should thrill our hearts!

Some respond by rejecting that reality. They reckon the Bible to be a document subject to their dissection and its teachings subject to their discretion. Judging the Bible to be little more than a collection of old myths and fables they distort, diminish, and disregard it. I know of what I speak because I was trained in the ways of mainline practices.

I lay much of the responsibility for the spiritual, moral, and civil decline of America at the feet of institutional mainline denominations. It is my observation that as goes the mainline, so goes the culture.

For more than a hundred years now, mainline ivory tower intellectuals and their theologically progressive disciples have been undermining the Biblical foundations of the Christian faith. They have whored out the Bride of Christ to other gods as if her purity did not matter and as if God were not a righteously jealous God. They have led people to do what is evil in the sight of the Lord, approving of that which the Bible clearly calls sin and elevating those engaged in sin into leadership. They actively suppress the Truth of God's Word in order to control the extraordinary institutional wealth amassed over generations of faithful giving.

The numeric membership decline of mainline denominations in the past fifty years has been precipitous, but great damage has been done and continues to be wrought by those who would undermine the Bible and assert in its place the gratification of the human imagination.

Mainline churches are shrinking: In the 1970s, about 30 percent of the U.S. population self-identified as part of mainline Christianity. By 2007, that number dropped to 18 percent. In 2014, 14.7 percent. In the last fifty years, the "six sisters" of Mainline Christianity lost half of their membership. And in the same span of time 25 percent of the population gave up belief in any faith at all. In fact, the rise of the "nones" or those unaffiliated with any religion became the largest religious group in the United States at the same rate as mainline denominations declined.[1] This gives you a picture of the changing landscape in our country and I lay the responsibility at the door of those who actively undermined the foundations of the faith and the faithful by teaching that the Bible is not the Word of God, but merely the words of men.

Once the foundation of the Bible was jettisoned, orthodox theological standards were sent tumbling. Every denomination has its own particular story, but suffice it to say, once a group thinks more highly of itself than it does of God's Word, the slope is more than slippery. The need for a Savior disappears if there is no sin other than that which is corporate and cultural. The power of the Spirit evaporates if there is no real supernatural will, no redemptive future toward which history is moving by God's design. There is no motivation to evangelize if all religious ideas are equally valid paths toward human fulfillment. Yes, this is what it has come to in mainline U.S. denominations. They still offer Vacation Bible School and Sunday School, baptism and the Communion; they still celebrate Christmas and Easter, but the stories are interpreted in ways you may not recognize as Christian. They still use the words *mission* and *evangelism* but they do not mean by those words going into all the world to make disciples through the proclamation of the Good News of the Gospel God offers to redeem individuals from the power and penalty of Sin through the atoning work of Jesus Christ. They are purveyors of a different gospel and we need to wake up to that reality.

We're talking specifically about the United Church of Christ (UCC), the Presbyterian Church USA (PCUSA), the Evangelical Lutheran Church in America (ELCA), the Episcopal Church (TEC), the Disciples of Christ, the American Baptist Churches, and the United Methodist Church (UMC)—unless they are able to do what none of the others have proven able to do and withstand the withering assault of the sexual revolutionaries within their governing authorities. And while it is true that faithful people and remnant congregations remain in each of these apostate denominations, the structures and the assets being deployed in social witness in the name of these denominations does not align with Biblical teaching on life, marriage, ordination, nor a litany of others issues.

The easiest way to describe the mainline is in contrast to what historically would have been called *fundamentalist* and is now broadly described as *evangelical Protestantism*. At one time the majority expression of Christianity in the United States, mainline Protestants are now a lengthening shadow. They share a progressive approach to social issues and they collect their voice in organizations like the National Council of Churches (NCC). In terms of doctrine, they describe the gospel in terms of liberation and social justice, and being on the right side of history means, for them, speaking on behalf of the marginalized.

The challenge is that institutionally and historically, there are no more educationally and socially privileged group of people in America than mainline Protestants. So although they now espouse very liberal theological and political views, they owned the means of the production and founded most of the country's elite colleges and universities. They are statistically wealthier, better educated, and over-represented in Congress when compared with other religious and non-religious Americans. So, although they espouse socialist ideologies for institutions, they tend to live privileged lives largely insulated from the systemic problems they now want the government to address.

Returning to the conversation specifically about the Bible, the United Church of Christ states it has no "rigid formulation of doctrine or attachment to creeds or structures," and it has the "breathing room to explore and hear" because God continues to speak.[2] The UCC has a statement of faith which can change at any given convening of its leadership and is therefore, not really a statement of faith at all.

Most people in the pews ask one question, "How did we get here?"

The really long and really short answer is: Sin. Questioning what God has said and whether or not God has said it, has its root in the Garden of the Eden but it comes to full flower in what is called the historical-critical method. Known as "higher criticism" this approach to the Bible seeks to understand the occasion of a particular book's writing and its meaning in its historical context. This is essential to a right understanding of what God has said. But many pursue higher criticism beyond this worthy goal and proceed to undermine the authenticity of the Bible as the Word of God.

Beginning in the late 1700s, Enlightenment imagineers thought so highly of Man they reconstructed a universe they believed to be devoid of God. But having effectively closed the system, recognizing naturalism alone, the question must be asked, "what about the Bible and the God to whom it attests?" If God does not exist or was limited to whatever force ignited the Big Bang, then the Bible, it was reasoned, is nothing more than a collection of myths, folk tales, and the chronicles of a particular people. Wandering far enough down this path you arrive at the place where the Bible is not the Word of God and, therefore, without any real authority.

Higher criticism is how we got here because if the Bible is merely the words of men then it has no greater authority than the words of men living today. That means not only the Bible but also the historic creeds and confessions have no authority in the life of the church. As denominations adopted this thinking, they not only stripped the Bible of its authority but undermined the authority of the Church as well. That led to divisions between warring factions looking to dominate seminaries, pulpits, and denominational billion-dollar endowments. In the end, if the thoughts of men today are as authoritative as the words in the Bible then there is no anchor, no compass, no boundary, no guide, and no God—beyond that which serves the individual in any given moment. Indeed, everyone does what is right in their own eyes. And the me believes itself to have vanquished Thee.

But we must not lose hope and we must never grow weary of doing good. We know the One who holds this moment and this day and this eon and all of eternity in the very palm of His holy hand. We are not alone; we have a Good Shepherd and we have the continual guidance of a Counselor and Comforter, the Holy Spirit. We also have the Word of God which He gives to serve as a lamp unto our feet and a light unto our path. The Word of God is still active and it still brings people to repentance in faith.

Lori Koch is an expert in global audio Bible engagement, who works for Faith Comes by Hearing. She shared a story with our radio show that still cuts me to the core.

She said:

> Some missionaries came to us from Haiti. They explained to us that 99% of the people they work with were illiterate. They can't read, but they have heard from the missionaries, "Man shall not live by bread alone but on every word that comes from the mouth of God." So what would they do? They would take a page from the printed Bible they can't

read and cut it up real small, put it in the soup and eat it.
They had such a longing to have God's Word in them.[3]

We should hear in their testimony echoes of Ezekiel 3 and Revelation 10. We should recall the words of the prophet Jeremiah who testifies to God, "Your words were found, and I ate them, and your words became to me a joy and the delight of my heart, for I am called by your name, O Lord, God of hosts" (Jeremiah 15:16). We should recall that Job considered the regular consumption of God's word as more necessary than food (23:10). The Psalmist considered it sweeter than honey and that which he desired more than gold (Psalm 19:10).

By contrast, in the United States, we have the Bible on our phones, on our shelves, and with a simple Google search we can find any verse we want, even if we cannot remember the reference. We throw good food in the trash when others are starving for just a taste that they might see that the Lord is good.

As my husband is fond of saying, "The Bible must be restored to its rightful place in the life of the Church if the Church is to be restored to her rightful place in the life of the culture." By that he means the Church has an appropriate redemptive role to play, but rejects both the Author's script and His direction. He's right. The Church is God's chosen agent of grace in the world today, populated by Christ's disciples. Those ministers of reconciliation and ambassadors of the Kingdom of Heaven, are to be gathered by the Church in order that they might be deployed as a force of God's revolutionary redemptive grace. The Church is also the place to which the broken and battered come for sanctuary and belonging whilst they remember anew who they are as image bearers and beloved children whom Christ died to redeem. The Church is currently serving neither role with any culture-wide effectiveness.

The divisions within the body of Christ in America bear continual public witness against every claim of the unity of the Spirit and the bond of peace produced by the presence of God's Spirit. So, either not everyone who claims the name of Christ in America is really a Christian, possessed of the Spirit of the living God, or, the spirit of the world has so fully infiltrated the American church that the institutions themselves need to be brought down in order for a righteous root to spring up. Whichever is the case, revival based on the Scriptures is needed.

How would this happen? That requires at least a two-part answer: one addressing liberals and another addressing evangelicals. For the Word of God to be restored to its rightful place in the life of the America's churches, liberals need to take it more seriously and evangelicals need to handle it more carefully.

Liberal and progressive Christians must submit anew to the authority of God and His self-revelation contained in the Scriptures. They must do as the Thessalonians are said to have done, "receive it for what it really is, the Word of God." Evangelicals, who acknowledge it as the Word of God, need to rightly handle it. There must be an unswerving loyalty to the meaning of the text regardless of the theological, denominational, or personal implications. Whatever the text demands must be dealt with honestly.

There must be a recommitment to valid hermeneutics as the process by which we discern what a text actually means not whatever we hope or imagine it means.

Complicating the divisions of the theological Right and Left is their over-identification with particular national political parties. For many Christians, faith no longer informs but is informed by politics. Articulating a distinctively Christian position when others in the conversation have already pre-judged what they expect the Christian position to be complicates the conversation.

This is just as great a problem on the political Left as it is on the political Right. The mainline Protestant Left, for example, fully aligns with the media's progressive view on every issue. And even though theologically and politically liberal pastors are far more likely to preach and advocate for partisan political candidates than conservative or evangelical pastors, the "religious Right" gets nearly all the negative press. Why is that? In a word: proximity.

Mainline Protestant pastors, theologians, seminaries, and people have played an outsized role in the formation of American political views from the beginning of our country. And over time, as those same denominations undermined their own Biblical foundations and followed after the gods of Marxist ideology and sexual revolutionaries, their outsized role has had deleterious effects. Indeed, as goes the mainline so goes the culture.

That's one reason the nostalgic call for a return to the *good ol' days* just won't do for those seeking to speak in an authentically Christian way on the issues of the day. You cannot simply point to a time when the kingdoms of this world, including the United States of America, reflected the reality of the Kingdom of God. No matter which period of history you choose, those *good ol' days* were only relatively good and only relatively good for a relative few. So the *good ol' days* for which we pine are usually days when "our kind" got their way over all the other kinds. That's a "kingdoms of this world" perspective and it's offensive to God.

I am appealing for a restoration of a distinctively Christian witness in America through a redemptive revolution of God's people based on the Word of God.

I propose a redemptive revolution led by God's people to make the Gospel visible, beautiful, and substantial. According to I Timothy 3:15 that's the role of the Church in the world.

Making the Gospel visible means we live *the* faith publicly. Note I did not say we live "our" faith publicly. *The* faith, once delivered to the saints, has content. It is not whatever syncretized system of cobbled-together ideas fit each individual's personal lifestyle preferences. *The* faith, rightly called Christian—worthy of the calling of Christ—

is a Gospel faith and that Gospel is the redemptive plan of God for all Creation. It encompasses all time and spans eternity. It includes, but is not limited to a person's apprehension of the saving grace of God offered in Jesus Christ unto salvation. The Gospel is bigger than most people have ever imagined. It is a revelation of the Kingdom of God.

What then does the Gospel and the Christian's Gospel calling look like in this twenty-first-century American life? How do we become reliable witnesses to the revealed truth of God's redemptive power in this post-truth pluralistic culture? What would that even look like? Casting the vision culture-wide, would look like the people of God advancing the Kingdom of God in every system, across every demographic and over every current dividing wall of hostility between us.

As the redemptive Gospel revolution advanced across the culture we would see individuals liberated from the power of Sin in life, restored relationships, redeemed marriages, racial reconciliation, and authentic justice. There would be an abundance of the kind of fruit described in Galatians 5: love, joy, peace, patience, kindness, goodness, gentleness, and self-control. The fruit we see now—vulgar language; perverse ideas; vile images; the degradation, objectification, and sub-jugation of people; and systemic injustice—would no longer flourish.

Again, the issue is not the fruit, but the root. Fruit is an outward sign an inward reality. Fruit is what Jesus uses as example of how to judge the human heart. You can know what's going on inside by what comes out.

We cannot fix what's broken in America by continuing to treat the symptoms without dealing with the root causes. It has been observed that the Holocaust didn't start with the extermination of millions of people in gas chambers, it started with words. But I con-tend even that does not get to the root of the problem. The words are a manifestation of thoughts which are an outgrowth of what's going on in the human heart.

The heart is at the heart of the matter. Not the physical blood-pumping organ in your chest, but the heart as the representation of a person's being, beliefs, affections, aspirations, hopes, and dreams. Again, this is not a new problem and this is not a distinctively American problem but we are reaping the harvest of what we have planted over time in the generations of American minds which is now ripe with rotten fruit.

In 1943, one man took on the education system in England by delivering a series of three lectures that became a book. The man was C.S. Lewis and the book is *The Abolition of Man*. Lewis noted that university students were arriving at Cambridge with not only perverse ideas, but wrong affections. Their hearts and minds had been trained in and toward the wrong things. In the opening chapter, Lewis famously says, "We make men without chests and expect from them virtue and enterprise. We laugh at honor and are shocked to find traitors in our midst."[4] That was seventy-five years ago.

The remaking of the human heart is God's specialty. He knows how to take a heart of stone and replace it with a heart of flesh. He knows how to write on the human heart and He knows how to break down the defensive walls we have constructed around our hearts.

But how do we even get our culture to the place where it knows it needs a heart transplant? First, we pray and then we publicly address Sin wherever we see it. And, yes, we have to call it what it is. Too often we have adopted the politically correct ways of the world instead of following the Biblical mandate to speak the truth in love.

It is time for God's people to speak God's Word, by God's Spirit, directly into the cultural conversations of the day. God alone has the right and the privilege of defining what is good and beautiful and true. Those transcendent values are the only legitimate basis for personal and public morality. But how do you help people see a cosmology when they've come to believe they are the captains of their own destiny?

Let's begin by making sure our worldview is correctly aligned with God's redemptive Gospel. Where shall we begin? Let's use the seemingly persistent issue of racism.

You may recognize the names of Bill and Vonette Bright. They started a ministry called Campus Crusade for Christ, now Cru. When you think of a couple who pressed the full force of their life together into advancing the cause of Christ in their generation, there is no better example than the Brights. Their legacy lives on in many of us and it lives in their own family as well. Their son Brad is married to Kathy, I quote here from her blog, DG4Kids, where she writes:

> "There's nothing wrong with racism ... " my husband told a black pastor in Washington D.C. They stared at each other for several uncomfortable seconds until Brad broke the silence, " ... unless the God of the Bible actually exists." The pastor's face lit up as the power of the statement sunk in. "Oh that's good! That's very good!" he said with a smile.
>
> The reality is, apart from God, morality is a fairy tale just like Santa Claus and the Easter Bunny! When Brad does radio shows he challenges anyone to call in and prove his statement wrong. Inevitably atheists will call and declare they don't believe in God but they're moral.
>
> Here's my husband's response: *I don't know you. You may very well adhere to moral standards. However, apart from the existence of God you can't explain to me why I'm obligated to treat you in a moral fashion.*
>
> We want our children to grow up with a strong moral compass. We want them to be honest, hard working, kind, generous, and extend love to all people. However, with the God of the Bible banned from the classroom and expelled from the public square it's no wonder the younger generations have a blurred sense of morality.

Bringing God back into the public debate is essential, but the best thing we can do for our children's future is to teach them who God really is and why it matters. Our homes are the most powerful change agent our country has.

... Remember, there's nothing wrong with lying, cheating, racism, homosexuality, drug abuse, pedophilia, abortion or rape ... unless the God of the Bible exists.[5]

Brad Bright is the person who taught me issues are never the issue. God is always the issue. He also taught me the power of reframing a conversation which moves the conversation from the issue at hand to the issue of God.

The issue is not just the rebel flag we fly but whether or not the ultimate banner over us is Jesus Christ.

The issue is not the color of our skin but the blood of the Body of Christ in which all have the offer of redemption.

The issue is not that some break laws and deserve justice but that all have sinned and fallen short of the glory of God.

The issue is not that an overwhelming number of kids are growing up in homes without dads but that they're not growing up in the household of God where they can be loved by Kingdom people.

The issue is not public education and a lack of mentors; the issue is discipleship.

The issue is not the culture but the current culture of the church.

Again, "There's nothing wrong with racism...unless the God of the Bible actually exists."

Q: Who is going to speak *that* truth (the Truth) authentically into the conversations of the day?

A: You and me.

And to do so, we must have lives saturated with the Word of God, full of grace and truth, and possessed not only of the mind of Christ but of His Spirit.

The restoration of the Word of God to its rightful place in the life of the Church begins with a restoration of the Word of God to its rightful place in the life of the believer. Transformed lives bear witness to the reality of the supernatural and reconnect the eternal with the everyday. So, let's get personal.

QUESTIONS FOR PERSONAL REFLECTION AND GROUP DISCUSSION

1. Do you receive the Bible as the word of God and, if not, why not?
2. To what do you attribute the decline of mainline Christianity in America over the past fifty years?
3. How has Christianity been over-identified with the partisan politics over the past generation?
4. How can a distinctively Christian voice differentiate from the Religious Right and the Religious Left?
5. What fruits have you fixated on instead of being concerned with the root?
6. What is the difference between being a hearer of the Word and a doer of it?
7. What issues do you see as issues instead of as people? What is God's perspective on the person? And then the issue?

CHAPTER 6

Yes, It's Personal
(and You Should Take It That Way)

Before we go any further into application, we have to pause. Because what we are about to discuss in the second half of the book hangs on one thing. If we are not personally gripped by the redeeming work of Jesus Christ, then none of it will make sense. So, is it personal for you?

Why is that important? Because the Gospel demands a response.

Those who receive Christ and believe in His name, the Bible tells us, become restored to their rightful relationship with God as children. That is the core identity of the Christian: child of God. Freed from the penalty of Sin, which is death, and freed from the power of Sin that enslaves in this life.

Part of the freedom that comes with the Gospel is the freedom to be selfless. Secure in the knowledge of who we, whose we are, where we're going, and what we're promised, Christians are liberated in ways the world simply does not comprehend. We can rejoice in suffering. We can accept adversity. We expect persecution. We can sing in prison. We see things differently.

Children of God are sons and daughters of the King, citizens of the Kingdom, co-heirs with Christ of glory. That totally reshapes how we view our role and time on earth. We're not trying to make a name for ourselves so much as make the name of Jesus known to others. We're not living for ourselves so much as offering our lives as living sacrifices for God to use as He wills. We're not living for the accumulation of wealth so much as we're seeking for our time, talent, and resources to be spent by God in ways that advance the Gospel.

I know, it sounds a little crazy and I suspect that is part of the point. As I Corinthians 1:18–31 reminds us:

> For the word of the cross is folly to those who are perishing, but to us who are being saved it is the power of God. For it is written,
>
> > "I will destroy the wisdom of the wise,
> > and the discernment of the discerning I will thwart."
>
> Where is the one who is wise? Where is the scribe? Where is the debater of this age? Has not God made foolish the wisdom of the world? For since, in the wisdom of God, the world did not know God through wisdom, it pleased God through the folly of what we preach to save those who believe. For Jews demand signs and Greeks seek wisdom, but we preach Christ crucified, a stumbling block to Jews and folly to Gentiles, but to those who are called, both Jews and Greeks, Christ the power of God and the wisdom of

God. For the foolishness of God is wiser than men, and the weakness of God is stronger than men.

Then Paul challenges us:

For consider your calling, brothers: not many of you were wise according to worldly standards, not many were powerful, not many were of noble birth. But God chose what is foolish in the world to shame the wise; God chose what is weak in the world to shame the strong; God chose what is low and despised in the world, even things that are not, to bring to nothing things that are, so that no human being might boast in the presence of God. And because of him you are in Christ Jesus, who became to us wisdom from God, righteousness and sanctification and redemption, so that, as it is written, "Let the one who boasts, boast in the Lord."

What does all that look like in the real world? I think sometimes we forget, this was written by a real guy who was really named Saul, who really became Paul. That real guy wrote a real letter to real Christians in a real town called Corinth. The issues they faced were the same real issues we face. The real questions they had remain the real questions real people have today. So much has changed and yet, so little. The Word of God is just as relevant and effective and powerful today as it was when it was first God-breathed through human instruments into written text. So the life of total submission to which the Bible calls the first Christians is no different than our calling today.

What does it look like today to lead a life worthy of the calling of Jesus Christ? If I could see my life in a mirror, would it look like that kind of life? If not, what in my life needs to be conformed to the image of Christ? Where does the goodness and truth of the Gospel need to further pervade my private thoughts, my public words, and my innermost beliefs? Where are my ideas, hopes, and desires out of alignment with the mind of Christ revealed in the Word of God?

Here we admit the Bible is full of hard teachings we'd rather rationalize away. But to do so is to set ourselves in judgment over God. This is the issue of authority we are facing in our own lives, in the church, and in the culture. It really is either "me or Thee" when it comes to authority. Either I recognize and joyfully submit to the reality that God is God (and I am not) or I set myself up as judge over God and His Word. That is the most basic form of idolatry and the root of all sin.

To be a Christian is to trust God and entrust ourselves to His goodness and grace. We face the reality that when we are in control things are out of control, so we turn the controls over to the One who knows how He designed it all to work in perfect harmony in the first place.

Galatians 2:20 captures this exchange when Paul says:

> I have been crucified with Christ. It is no longer I who live, but Christ who lives in me. And the life I now live in the flesh I live by faith in the Son of God, who loved me and gave himself for me.

What does Paul mean when he says, "it is no longer I who live, but Christ who lives in me"? He tells us in the following sentence, "The life I now live in the flesh, I live by faith in the Son of God." This exchange remains a mystery to most people, but this is the essential exchange that takes place when a person accepts the sacrifice of Christ upon the cross and gives Him their life to be lived in the world now. So, if you are in Christ—covered by Him—and Christ is in you—animating your new life in the Spirit—then you are dead and He's alive.

This is so contrary to the way we've been taught to think in self-centric America that it helps to remember that the Gospel is for the whole world and all time. The Gospel and the Church are not exclusively nor even preferentially "American," so you may have to sort out what is distinctively Christian in your worldview and what is basic Americana.

The American ideals of being self-made, pulling yourself up by your bootstraps and doing it "my way," are cultural, but they are not Christian. Christians recognize we are not self-made nor are we self-rising. Jesus actually came to do for us what we could never do for ourselves and "my way" was precisely the wrong way when the One Way of Jesus was the only right way.

For as *Christian* as we imagine American culture to be, living a distinctively Christian life in America today proves to be very counter-cultural.

- The culture glorifies the self but the Christian has died to self and lives to glorify God
- The culture deifies personal autonomy but the Christian surrenders control to God
- The culture celebrates individual identity but the Christian finds their identity in Christ
- The culture places its hope in the change promised by politicians and government but the Christian anchors their hope to Jesus who changes everything

The witness of the Christian in the world is a witness of one who:

- Finds joy and purpose in the exaltation of another
- Puts the Gospel on display by living in the world, but not of it

- Lives as a citizen of the Kingdom of Heaven amidst the kingdoms of this world
- Proclaims that the hope of the world is found in the person of Jesus and lives with their life so fixed on Him that others cannot help but wonder

Our Christian witness is as much in our living as Jesus as it is in our actual preaching of Jesus. Being a Christian is an identity; it is a calling, it is a way of life, it is a mission, and it is a post. It informs and influences every part of life: how we think, what we watch, what we buy, how we work, who we date/marry, how we relate to others, how we parent, how we vote, what we expect from government, how we serve, how we spend our money, and what we say in conversation.

It always helps to have an objective lesson. So here's my show and tell: Joni Eareckson Tada. She's the founder of a ministry called Joni and Friends International Disability Center. It's a non-profit ministry with an incredible global reach.

She is an international advocate for people with disabilities and, I would say, she is probably the most recognizable Christian on the forefront of these discussions year in and year out. She suffered a diving accident in 1967 that left her a quadriplegic and she's been in a wheelchair ever since. She provides Christ-centered programs to special needs families as well as training to churches. Joni and Friends serves thousands of special needs families through family retreats. They've actually delivered a hundred thousand wheelchairs and Bibles to needy disabled people in developing nations.

But, all the incredible work of her organization is just part of the reason she is a hero of the faith for me. Her work is an extension of the way she lives out the Gospel in her daily life. She shared this incredible story on *The Reconnect* that explains more of what I mean:

I served on the National Council on Disability when the Americans with Disabilities Act was authored, drafted, and then it was signed into law and I'll never forget being on the South lawn at the White House watching President Bush sign the ADA into law and after the signing ceremony we went back to the Hyatt Regency for a reception and the director of our National Council on Disability wanted to propose a toast and, Carmen, this is what he said. It was amazing.

He said, "You know, this law is great in that it now removes discriminatory policies in hiring people with disabilities. That's great, and this law is also wonderful in that it provides more access into public accommodations like restaurants, and this act is great in that one day buses all across America will have mechanical lifts" and then he said, "But this law is not gonna change the employer's heart. This law is not going to change the heart of the waiters at the restaurant. This law is not gonna change the bus driver's heart," and then he looked at his glass and said, "Here's to changed hearts."

Carmen, by that point I was in tears because that is our job. You and I as Christians, our listeners today, we are the ones who have the message, the gospel message that changes peoples' hearts, not just toward people with disabilities, but to anyone with whom we might have some kind of difference and I have seen incredible progress in the church in the year since the ADA has been passed because the church is responding to a higher law than the ADA. They're responding to the law of God that says we are to reach out and honor the needy. We are to help the defenseless. We are to befriend the widow and the orphan, take care of the afflicted and slowly I am seeing churches now in America and overseas just doing an amazing work in showcasing the mercy of God towards special needs families.[1]

That's it. Right there. We are the ones called day-to-day to show-case the goodness and beauty of the Gospel. Because when that good-ness and beauty gets into our own lives and begins to transform us, it flows out.

That is the kind of conviction I want to be true in my life. All the laws and the programs and the culture wars in the world will never be as powerful as the personal representation of the Gospel in the life of the Christian. It's actually how Jesus designed it when he commis-sioned his rag-tag group of followers to go into all the world and make disciples. Good Lord, what a plan!

Joni is what I would call a Galatians 2:20 person.

If you're not a Galatians 2:20 person, I want you to consider becoming one. Because, the Galatians 2:20 person lives with the knowledge of the reality that they are already dead. There is literally nothing the world can do. What do we have to fear if we've already been crucified with Christ? (And yes, by grace, Galatians 2:20 people are also alive again, new creations, raised with Christ and living for Christ.) That is liberty.

If we are living a Galatians 2:20 life, then we become representa-tives for Jesus everywhere we go. In His Spirit, we become agents of God's grace in the world. Not agents of a thing, or agents of a transac-tion, but agents of God. Once we see ourselves rightly, as ambassadors of God's Kingdom and agents of Grace, ministers of reconciliation and representatives of Christ, we are people on a mission and it's advancing every day.

We can be thankful we do not have to sit and wonder what that means. The Bible is as straightforward and clear as one can get about what it looks like to be a representative of Christ. Second Corinthians 5:16–21 says,

From now on, therefore, we regard no one according to the flesh. Even though we once regarded Christ according to the flesh, we regard him thus no longer. Therefore, if anyone is in Christ, he is a new creation. The old has passed away; behold, the new has come. All this is from God, who through Christ reconciled us to himself and gave us the ministry of reconciliation; that is, in Christ God was reconciling the world to himself, not counting their trespasses against them, and entrusting to us the message of reconciliation. Therefore, we are ambassadors for Christ, God making his appeal through us. We implore you on behalf of Christ, be reconciled to God. For our sake he made him to be sin who knew no sin, so that in him we might become the righteousness of God.

Put simply, God's grace changes everything. Everything old is gone, and grace remains. Our new life in Christ is what's real.

It is critical we get this. Because God makes His appeal on earth through us.

The gift of a new life we have received is not just for us. God wants to reconcile the *whole* world to Himself—and He is using His people to make that appeal. This means our appeal is not a "community" not a "feeling" but God. The very King and Creator of the Universe. The enormity of that calling is what He has entrusted to us. Nothing less.

Reread the passage above and note the opening sentence. Typically, when reading the Bible, when we see a "therefore," we ask, what's it there for? It points us back to a preceding revealed truth. So what is the truth that makes us change how we view people—no longer just as flesh but as souls for reconciliation to God?

Directly preceding this well-known passage is this: "For the love of Christ controls us, because we have concluded this: that one has died for all, therefore all have died; and he died for all, that those who live might no longer live for themselves but for him who for their sake died and was raised."

That sounds a lot like Galatians 2:20. The reason we are ambassadors, the reason we are given the ministry of reconciliation all comes back to the fact that if we are in Christ Jesus, we are no longer our own. The lordship, the control, of our life is handed over to the only one who is worthy of it. The one who died in our place, for our sins.

If you read the Bible you'll come to see that this Galatians 2:20, I Corinthians 5:14 message starts to sound repetitive. And when the Bible says things more than once we have to remember that means God is repeating Himself.

Every time I hear that echo of repeated commands I recall the times my mother had to repeat things throughout my growing up years. "Carmen Suzette, how many times do I have to tell you?" I remember distinctly the last time she said it because of what I said back, "I guess at least one more." There's a reason it was the last time she ever had to repeat herself because the lesson was reinforced in ways that changed my attitude and my behavior. I confess the memory of disrespecting my precious mother stings to this day. But then I realize I sass God just as badly. When God repeats something, it may be an indication He knows it is something we need to hear again because we have failed to submit.

Ugh. Yes, there's that word: submission. It goes against our nature to give up control and yet if we know God then we know He knows better about everything. The Christian life cannot be lived under our control. The only way to live an authentically Christian life is through the very unnatural (supernatural) control of the Holy Spirit. The life of a Christian is one of surrender. The initial surrender is the moment of repentance when we die to self and give it all to God but there is also a moment by moment surrender every day as we yield our will to His.

The ministry of reconciliation must be personal for us before we can take it to the culture at large.

We know what we *need* but *how*?

We have identified the problem in chapter five: rotten fruit resulting from a compromised witness rooted in gospels other than The Word of God. So, the solution is a restoration of the Word of God to its rightful place in the life of the Church (read: every believer) in order that the Church can rightfully influence the culture. Kingdom people living by Kingdom principles in the midst of the kingdoms of this world.

The how to:

1. *Receive the Word of God for what it really is: the word of God.* I Thessalonians 2:13 reveals this first step in an honest engagement with God. If you're not willing to be honest and deal honestly with God, the communication ends with your rejection of His self-revelation. This involves reverence: we do not receive the Word of God in order to manipulate it for our purposes, but to honor God and His purpose in giving it.

2. *Respond to the Word of God for who He really is.* This is repentance and followership. If Jesus really is who the Bible says He is then that changes everything because Jesus changes everything. Rightly responding to Jesus as Lord brings about a full reorientation of the thoughts of the mind, the affections of the heart, and the priorities of life.

3. *Represent the Word of God in ways consistent with its content and character.* This is done through the moment by moment living of a transformed life in the midst of the real world. This is also the ambassadorial or ministerial nature of the Christian faith. In order to rightly represent the Word there must be a valid interpretation

of what God has actually said and then integrity to that interpretation in our lives and life together. Jesus didn't come as the Word of God incarnate to make us pious, but in order that we might be restored to right and righteous relationship to the Father. Any preacher pandering to the itchy ears or personal proclivities of contemporary culture is misrepresenting the Word's content and character and should be called out.

Fair warning

The world does not like the message of surrender and the world takes it out on the messengers. We should not be surprised when what God tells us to expect comes to pass. We should get used to being called names, charged with being politically incorrect, or accused of standing on the wrong side of history. Jesus experienced far worse for us. We should come to expect the unbelieving world will be hostile toward those who are aligned with a Lord it does not acknowledge and a God it rejects. We should expect negative things to be hurled in our direction—insults and all manner of hateful speech.

But when people are taking pot shots at us, we recognize the real target of their rage is Jesus. They are really aiming at Him. We must recognize that the flaming arrows of the evil one might be aimed in our direction in this lifetime, but Jesus is the One who takes the blows. I want to encourage you to have hope in that fact and take the insults that come your way with honor for Him.

Yes, Christians get depressed and we grow discouraged, but we do not despair of the realities of living as people of faith in a fallen world. That's our calling. That's the context of the Great Commission. That, dear brothers and sisters, is why we're still here: that the world might see through us to Him.

It is time we take hold of that for which Christ Jesus took hold of us. It's time we became more like Philly Jesus. Who is Philly Jesus? He is a recovering heroin addict, who now walks the streets of Philadelphia dressed as Jesus might have in the first century. In the most literal way possible, he is seeking to represent Jesus to the people of Philadelphia. We chuckle at him, but he's a provocative character in the conversation about counter-cultural Christianity and living our calling to show forth Christ to others.

I am not advocating you go put on first-century garb, but we need the kind of mind-shift that takes off the world and puts on Christ—without that, our Christianity is nothing but a put-on.

When we become Christians, we become representations of Jesus to the world. Until it becomes *that* personal and real, our hope to influence culture is going to be a fleshly mission carried out through human means. We will be missing the mark and exhausted, frustrated and angry doing it.

I advocate we taste and see again that the Lord is good. That we savor the Savior. Trust me, if you meditate on the goodness of God, if you revel in His Grace, if you fix your eyes on His beauty you will not be able to stop talking about Him. Like a person who has just fallen in love, you will sing the praises of the Lover of your soul.

We all know "that person" who can't stop talking about their favorite sports team or their favorite coffee shop. They are evangelists for that which they love. In that sense, we are all evangelists for something. What I'm advocating is that we become anew what we are: people who—like the Samaritan woman at the well or the Gerasene demoniac or the leper in Capernaum—literally cannot keep the good news to ourselves.

If your mind is protesting, "but what will people think?" hold that thought because you're onto something! It's a great question. And I say, "Let's give them something to think about!"

Philippians 4:8 says, "Whatever is true, whatever is honorable, whatever is just, whatever is pure, whatever is lovely, whatever is commendable, if there is any excellence, if there is anything worthy of praise, think about these things." So, what will people think about after an encounter with us? Will they think on these things? If we have done our job in representing Christ then they will be looking at Him and their mindset will begin to change as they allow who He is to penetrate the defenses of their heart and mind.

I cannot explain how it happens, but it happens. If a person will simply fix their eyes on Jesus and look full in His wonderful face they will find that the wind and the waves stop howling, the peace which passes human understanding fills their life. Do all the issues of the world pass away? No, but as Paul said, "I know the secret of being content no matter the circumstances."

If we know the secret it's time to share it with a very discontent world.

QUESTIONS FOR PERSONAL REFLECTION AND GROUP DISCUSSION

1. Probe the question at the beginning of this chapter, "Is the Gospel personal for you?"
2. A Galatians 2:20 person is like Paul, already dead to self and alive to Christ. What does that look like in the real world? Who is a Galatians 2:20 person in your life?
3. The words submission and surrender are central to this chapter. What do those words mean and how are they counter-cultural?
4. There's a biting question at the end of the chapter: Have you put on Christ or is your Christianity just a put-on? What does that question seek to unmask about some self-identified Christians today?

_____

_____

_____

_____

_____

_____

_____

_____

_____

_____

_____

_____

CHAPTER 7

The Call to Look Up, Suit Up, and Speak Up

I heard him murmur, "What's wrong with the world?" I could have ignored the comment and I could have ignored him. I had my own table, my own coffee, my own work. I could have, but I couldn't. I couldn't stop myself from glancing over to see what provoked him to ask one of the ultimate questions. He was reading something on his iPad. I couldn't see it. I looked at him intently, with interest and compassion, and asked, "What now?"

He looked up and with only a moment's hesitation shared the latest horror story passing as news across his social media feed. It was not the kind of news anyone ever wants to hear and yet it is the kind of news we hear every day. After giving me the gist of the latest version of man's inhumanity to man, he asked again with a sense of grief and anger and total defeat, "What's wrong with the world?" Then he added, "What's wrong with us?"

Wide open door. I uttered a brief silent prayer and, without moving any closer physically, I engaged in one of the deepest conversations I've ever had with another person.

"You're asking a really big question and I think it has a really big answer—but let me ask you first, are you okay?"

You see, the issues of the world are what they are and the propositional answers related to God and the cosmos and Creation and the fall and redemption through Christ are all incredibly important. But sitting before me was a person who was broken and grieving and, I suspected, lost. Turning on the high beams and giving him the double barrel "Truth that surpasses all understanding" might have just driven him further back into the woods.

His eyes fell and within seconds so did the tears. He was so desperate to talk that he would talk to anyone, even a complete stranger in a coffee shop. His story flowed: his wife left him and took his little girl, and he didn't have the money for a good attorney. He felt like a failure and his work was suddenly meaningless and his friends were telling him to get revenge, but he loved her and he just wanted her back. His "what's wrong with the world" was not so much about what was going on *out there* but a recognition of the wrongness of the world deep inside, *right here.*

I don't have the answers to all those questions, but I had an hour to listen and I let him process. My goal was to get him reconnected to some sources of hope. I asked strategic questions that led him to make two calls: one to his dad, who he'd been too embarrassed to call, but was exactly the person he needed. The other call was to a guy he'd known in college who was a Christian and lived in the next town. I didn't lead him to the Lord, but I bore faithful witness to the reality of God who cares and consoles and counsels and offers hope.

I have no idea what happened. I don't even know his name. I received it as a divine appointment I was faithful to keep. I trust the dozens of other Christians that man has encountered since—and the Christians his wife was encountering on that same day—were equally faithful to their calling.

This chapter bridges the gap between knowing and doing. Many Christians are hearers of the Word but not doers of it. We are actually called to acknowledge God always and in all ways—not only on some days and in some ways. So, why don't we? What are we so afraid of? That we might make a fool of ourselves or be rejected? Jesus has that covered.

When we think about having conversations with people we already know, some of whom are in the church, we must recognize that some of the barriers that need to be torn down are institutional religious traditionalism, formalized ritualism, and cultural relativism. But on the personal level there are also layers of cynicism, doubt, defeatism, and worldly thinking that are contrary to the calling of presenting the truth accurately, substantively, and winsomely in whatever context we find ourselves. This is labor for which we must prepare ourselves spiritually, intellectually, and emotionally. So, let's get to it!

Hey! Look up!

Wake up! Look out! Heads up!

"This is your wake-up call," the voice on the other end of the line said at 3:42 a.m.

"I didn't ask for a wake-up call," I responded.

"You were scheduled to receive a wake-up call at 3:45 a.m., would you like me to call back then?"

"No," I nearly yelled, now fully awake. "I didn't schedule a wake-up call," I repeated, hoping that would bring an end to this exchange.

"Well, I wonder who I'm supposed to be waking up?" a genuinely confused voice asked no one.

I let out a long sigh. "I don't know, but I'm awake now. Thanks for calling."

I didn't ask to be awoken but now that I'm up...

It was the practice of Jesus to get up early in the morning to pray. Mark 1:35 describes Him "rising very early in the morning, while it was still dark," Mark tell us Jesus "went out to a desolate place, and there He prayed." Have you ever wondered why?

I remember when my friend Betty told me that after her son died she made it a practice to get up in the dark, go to the eastern facing window which was in the dining room of her home, and wait. She said, "I couldn't pray. I didn't doubt God's love but I didn't understand what was going in my life. I did the only thing I could think of; I got up before the sun just to watch it rise." When life is dark, Creation bears witness to the reality that hope is on the horizon. The sun rises.

Betty told me about the day her mourning turned to laughter. "I was sitting in the same chair, wrapped in the same worn afghan, wearing the same robe, looking mournfully out the same window when it happened. The first rays of the sun came over the horizon and the ice in my heart thawed. Hope returned. It was my Easter morning and I began to laugh at my own despair."

She said in hindsight the valley of the shadow of death seems much less deep and far less long than when you're in it. "When you're headed into it with someone you love or headed back out of it after they've gone, the valley of the shadow of death seems more death than shadow. But once you're out again, on the hilltop, looking back from a place of light, you see that it is only a shadow. And then of course you see that you were also never really as alone as you felt."

That is the Twenty-Third Psalm in the lived testimony of a mom who buried her son.

When did your wake-up call come? When did you realize Jesus was really the Savior and really wanted to restore your relationship with God? What's your story of getting up in the dark and being transformed by the reality of the rising Light?

Too often we're so consumed with our own concerns we fail to be awake to all the concerns of the people around us. Look around. Yes, right now. Look around. What are the circumstances of the lives of the people around you? Who are these people? Who is alone? Who is struggling financially? Who is trying to be someone they are not? Who is confused about their real identity? Who are you tempted to avoid because you can tell their life is a mess? From whom are you tempted to avert your gaze and bypass because honestly, who wants to step in all that? Short answer: Jesus.

Jesus, knowing full well what He was getting into, gave up the glory of heaven for the mess of the human experience—not because He needed to experience what it's like to be human, but so we could see God. He condescended to our reality and by the power of His indwelling Spirit, He sends us to go and do likewise. And right now, you and I are Jesus' people, His agents of grace, His ministers of reconciliation, His presence to that person who is struggling, confused, hurting, lost, or sitting alone in the dark with no hope that the sun will ever rise on their situation.

Jesus wants to lean into that person's life and He's got you in proximity! In the age-old game of tag, "you're it!"

Now, before you admit internally or externally you don't want to be right where you are, in proximity to that messy person, think of all the harder places you might be. Consider what it's like for those who do not know the saving grace of God and the secret of being content no matter the circumstances of this life.

"He chose the darkness," Marie sobbed. "Our kids, our life…he chose the darkness." She could have been telling me about a descent into drugs or alcohol or porn or gambling but in this case the descent into the darkness was the gay lifestyle. Marie saw her husband through career changes and a serious illness that nearly took his life. He saw that second chance as an opportunity to be someone else, live another life, unshackled from the demands of being a husband and father and son. He gave up contact with everyone in his former life, including me. Marie wanted to know what she did wrong, "I prayed, I supported him, we have a beautiful home, our kids are great," her voice trailed off. She didn't mention that she works full-time and is a stunning human being herself, but those things are true as well. "I don't want to be divorced," she added, "it's all so dark."

These are the conversations where reliance upon God to speak is paramount. Marie was fragile and wounded and scared and angry. I wanted to assure her without offering meaningless platitudes. While it was certainly true God had all this and God would care for her and her children and God would make a way and would ultimately use this for good, none of those things were the right thing to say right at that moment. The right thing to do was to be present. The ministry of presence is a powerful witness. The incarnation, remember, is itself an act of showing up.

Sometimes all we can do is be present with another person in their pain. Think here of Job's friends. They showed up, which is great, but then they spoke up. They did not speak truth into his life and they did not bear witness to the grace of God. That's a fail. Telling someone we don't know what to say, but we are there for them is a great gift. Indeed, your presence is a present to a person bereft.

In terms of Biblical examples of people who lived as Kingdom-advancing ambassadors in and through very difficult circumstances, among my favorites are Joseph, Daniel, and Paul.

Joseph, sold into slavery by his brothers, falsely accused and imprisoned, rose through adversity to a position of significance in Egypt and was used by God to sustain the lineage of God's people who were facing famine. His operating system was not the way of the world but the counsel of God.

Daniel's story is not unlike Joseph's. Daniel was raised in what we must assume was a devout Jewish family of some means and education. Daniel was chosen by the Babylonians to be taken into exile to serve directly in the King's court because Daniel was quite evidently a very fine young man.

We think of him from the story of the lion's den, but Daniel's full story is worth exploring. Daniel personifies what it looks like to be God's person in every place, at every time, under every circumstance, no matter what.

I think we forget Daniel was a prisoner of war. From a worldly point of view, Daniel had a horrible life. His parents were very likely killed. His homeland was conquered. He was taken captive as a slave and most likely castrated. He would never have a wife. He would never father a child. He would never own a home. Why not eat, drink, and enjoy whatever privileges might come to those who did whatever the king wanted, whenever he wanted it? Because Daniel knew who he was, where he came from, why he was alive, and where he was going when he died. Daniel lived as a representative of the Kingdom of God in the midst of the very fallen kingdoms of this world.

Then there is the apostle Paul. When we read his letters to the churches we often forget many of them were written from prison. Paul had no wife, no children, and no legacy the world would credit as worthy. And yet, Paul counted it all joy. Paul advanced the Gospel always in all ways. Paul viewed every encounter—with a jailer or a sailor or a guard or a governor—as an opportunity to advance the Gospel. Every direction he looked he saw opportunity. Those are the eyes of Christ on the world.

Look around you, scan the headlines, survey the city, the nation, the world. What do you see? You are alive right now because God intends to use you as an agent of His grace in the midst of the world

He so loves. God can use you where you are, knowing what you know, having experienced what you have experienced to accomplish His glory. If you're as old as Abraham or as young as Daniel, if you're as compromised as Rahab or have a life as hard as the Samaritan woman Jesus met at the well, God can send you as a redeemed ambassador of the Kingdom of God to bear light in the kingdoms of this world.

It will not be easy. You may not get to be around to see the fruit. It runs completely counter to everything the world says matters. And it's an inexhaustible well of joy that springs up each new day with the certain knowledge you are doing what you were always made to do for the glory of the only One in the universe who ultimately matters. Unexplainable? Yes. But also undeniable.

Think of it this way: you are putting flesh on the Gospel today. As you are in Christ and Christ is in you, as you bring the mind of Christ to bear on the matters of the day, other people get to experience the peace of His mind. It may not be what they thought they wanted or needed, but when they experience it, they want more.

Jesus did not address issues, He allowed His life to intersect with the lives of others and in those moments, through those transforming encounters, people were radically changed.

When the mind of Christ is our operating system and the Spirit of Christ is in control, the world not only looks different, we are different in it. That changes everything. That changes how we see other people, our circumstances and the opportunities to glorify God.

Regular people with regular challenges, living regular lives, came to live differently after they encountered Jesus. Did all their troubles magically cease? No. Did all poverty vanish? No. Was all sickness healed? No. Was the tyranny of an oppressive government overthrown? No. Did the practice of slavery come to an end? No. Did they get out of paying taxes? No. It is not about how God might change our circumstance, but how God changes us in the midst of it.

We have infinitely more power than we access and infinitely more influence than we use. What difference would it make for you to intentionally engage with the people who are working on challenges like those listed above? I don't know, but I know when an ambassador from the Kingdom of Heaven is present, the conversation changes. People are treated with greater dignity. Words are less coarse. Proposals are more generous. Generative solutions are more numerous. Why? Because the Spirit of God is brought to bear and the spirit of the world is pressed down. The principle is simple and true: darkness cannot remain when light enters. The call is to go and be shiny.

Here's a question: What if, instead of issues, we saw people?

Most of Jesus' earthly ministry happened "as he was going" or "along the way." Yes, His face was set toward the Cross but He never treated anyone as an interruption as He headed there.

Jesus allowed people to overhear him pray.

He allowed people to catch a glimpse of glory.

He was constantly comparing and contrasting the kingdom of the world with the Kingdom of God.

He wanted people to taste and see that the Lord is good.

How can we do the same?

How can we mentor someone or shadow someone to gain proximity and time and opportunity?

Where can we invite a group to gather to talk about what's going on in the world and what God thinks about it all?

Who needs a blessing?

Note that as Jesus engaged the world He did so in ways that always and in all ways honored the Father in heaven. It is a great challenge for us to do likewise. We want to engage the battle with the weapons of this world and we want to slay the enemies of the Cross. But those people are not the enemy. They may be deluded, confused, captive, but they are not the enemy. The goal of engagement is redemption, not annihilation. And we can never engage the world for the Gospel in non-Gospel ways.

Suit up

So, how do we engage in ways that honor Jesus? Certainly we have Jesus himself as our exemplar but we also have instructive texts like Ephesians 6:1–20.

> Finally, be strong in the Lord and in the strength of his might. Put on the whole armor of God, that you may be able to stand against the schemes of the devil. For we do not wrestle against flesh and blood, but against the rulers, against the authorities, against the cosmic powers over this present darkness, against the spiritual forces of evil in the heavenly places. Therefore take up the whole armor of God, that you may be able to withstand in the evil day, and having done all, to stand firm. Stand therefore, having fastened on the belt of truth, and having put on the breastplate of righteousness, and, as shoes for your feet, having put on the readiness given by the gospel of peace. In all circumstances take up the shield of faith, with which you can extinguish all the flaming darts of the evil one; and take the helmet of salvation, and the sword of the Spirit, which is the word of God, praying at all times in the Spirit, with all prayer and supplication. To that end, keep alert with all perseverance, making supplication for all the saints, and also for me, that words may be given to me in opening my mouth boldly to proclaim the mystery of the gospel, for which I am an ambassador in chains, that I may declare it boldly, as I ought to speak.

On whose strength—strength of personality, strength of will, strength of wisdom, strength of ideas, strength of wit, strength of prowess—are you relying?

What or whose armor are you wearing right now and to what end? From God's perspective, you need His armor. And all you're expected to do is stand.

Q: Stand where?

A: In His armor.

Q: For what?

A: His glory.

Q: Against what?

A: The schemes of the Devil.

Now, if as you read that, you think to yourself, "there isn't really a devil." Stop and ask yourself why you think that. What leads you to believe God has lied in the Bible about the existence of the Devil from Genesis through Revelation? What leads you to believe that although Jesus acknowledged the reality of the Devil, you don't have to? What makes you think that if Jesus was tempted by the Devil, you won't be?

If you do acknowledge the reality of an ultimate Enemy and you accept God's revelation that says the Enemy is warring over every human soul, that he's crafty, prowling around constantly looking for a way to destroy and devour people, can you see that most people you meet are his prey? They are prisoners of war who have lived so long in the Enemy's camp their natural instinct is now very base: fight or flight, selfish, desperate, and dark. They do not know who they are. They do not understand this is not all there is. They have no sense of hope beyond whatever they can sensually experience or accumulate.

It may be far from your experience but it is important to understand many people we encounter have absolutely no sense of God whatsoever. They have no sense of the supernatural. They are so desperate to feel something they equate pain with pleasure as long as it stimulates the senses. Over time, they become increasingly numb and need deeper or stronger or more potent sensate experiences. The Bible describes it as having lost all sensitivity. Paul observes in Ephesians 4:19 "They have become callous and have given themselves up to sensuality, greedy to practice every kind of impurity." Does that sound like the world today?

What then are we to do? Isolate and insulate ourselves? No. As the first generation of Christians was called to engage, so too are we.

Ephesians 4 goes on to say in verses 25–32, "let each one of you speak the truth with his neighbor, for we are members one of another. Be angry and do not sin; do not let the sun go down on your anger, and give no opportunity to the Devil."[1]

Speak up

We are called to speak the truth with our neighbors. That is engagement. And yes, it's okay to get righteously indignant when we see and hear and read about the gross violations of dignity taking place all over the world. But, what do we do with that anger? We do not sin, we do something with it immediately and we do not allow the devil to use our anger nor its provocation to get us off track from our calling.

Ephesians chapter 4 ends with instruction about how we should engage as Christians who are in the world but not of it:

> Let no corrupting talk come out of your mouths, but only such as is good for building up, as fits the occasion, that it may give grace to those who hear. And do not grieve the Holy Spirit of God, by whom you were sealed for the day of redemption. Let all bitterness and wrath and anger and clamor and slander be put away from you, along with all malice. Be kind to one another, tenderhearted, forgiving one another, as God in Christ forgave you.

Let's practically apply that in a conversation you might have with your actual neighbor. Every situation is unique and yet every situation is also exactly the same. You are present as God's representative. You have been redeemed. You know the Truth which sets us ultimately free. You have been forgiven and you have been taught by grace to be gracious. Why would you engage with the weapons of the world like bitterness, wrath, anger, slander or gossip? Why would you resort to cutting sarcasm or degrading dysphemisms? Take joy in the position you have! You can be magnanimous in this (and every) situation because you know this is not all there is, you know to get one up on someone here and now is a pyrrhic victory when the actual war being waged is over your neighbor's soul.

That perspective changes everything. That was the perspective of God related to you and me and it is God's perspective on everyone we will ever meet who does not yet know Jesus.

Does the preservation of your property line matter? Yes. But only to a point. Is it more important you win a temporal battle about the placement of a fence or that you win the opportunity to remain in relationship with your neighbor who is currently on the wrong side of the ultimate fence?

Yes, we are called to speak truth, but in love.

Yes, we are called to engage, but in ways that honor Jesus.

Yes, we are called to fight for what's right, but not with the weapons of the world.

This spirit of engagement is captured in II Timothy 2:23–26 which reads,

> Have nothing to do with foolish, ignorant controversies; you know that they breed quarrels. And the Lord's servant must not be quarrelsome but kind to everyone, able to teach, patiently enduring evil, correcting his opponents with gentleness. God may perhaps grant them repentance leading to a knowledge of the truth, and they may come to their senses and escape from the snare of the devil, after being captured by him to do his will.

God knows sometimes people are just looking for a fight. That's not the posture of a servant of the Lord. We are not quarrelsome. We are not going to engage in quarrels. We are also not going to run away nor be silent. This passage makes clear that we're supposed to remain engaged, ready to offer information and correction while enduring what is described as "evil." We are engaging with worldly people, possessed of the spirit of the age, and we're on their turf.

They are likely to remind us of our strangeness. They will call us fools. They will see if we can be scared off or baited into the kind of fight they want to have.

That's why putting on the full armor of God is so imperative! We need protection and we also need precision spiritual instruments that pierce the soul and cut to the heart. Indeed, "God may perhaps grant them repentance leading to a knowledge of the truth, and they may come to their senses and escape from the snare of the Devil," and YOU might be the agent of His grace who is standing right there when it happens.

Cultural engagement is too big to get our arms around. But a conversation with an individual who sees the world differently than we see it, a person who is so captive to the spirit of the world they cannot even see their own enslavement—we can get our arms around that. We engage the culture by engaging in conversation with individuals. And we do so in a way that honors Jesus because it's not about us; it's ultimately all about Him.

Sometimes, it is helpful to think about some practical ways to step into a conversation, so the next time you are at the neighborhood BBQ or book club, you are prepared to seize the opportunity. Here are a few practical ways to get started:

- **Open the door by asking a question** that helps you understand the background, experiences, triumphs, and tragedies that have shaped the life or worldview of the person with whom you are conversing. People want to be understood, to know they are known and they matter. They will not be persuaded to engage if all you seem interested in is making your argument and hammering your point. Remember who you are, an ambassador, and remember who they are, a precious person.

- **Humility, humility, humility.** Take a posture of humility from the very start. The model here is the incarnation of Jesus Christ. He didn't need to get down on our level to understand us but so we could understand God. Our model is Jesus—and He is radically humble.

- **Be willing to repent.** Some people have been deeply wounded by their prior experiences. You are not accountable for things done by others, but you do represent Christ who took on our sin as His own so we might be reconciled to God. Certainly, if applicable, apologize for what you did or failed to do in the past. But be prepared to help them through a wrong not yours to confess. Genuine remorse is uncommon today and you can be a healing agent of grace in the life of the other.

  One warning: do not get down into the pit of despair with someone. You are holding fast to the tree of life. You are connected to the redemptive reality of God. Do not allow yourself to be dragged repeatedly into a pity party nor down into the pit a self-destructive person may be digging. You are there to lift up, not be pulled down.

- **Speak with the dignity, diplomacy, and authority of an ambassador by:**
  - **Establishing common ground.** Remember the idea of ground rules? Well, conversations today need ground rules. It is important these be identified, articulated, and mutually agreed upon so you can hold one another mutually accountable if things start to go sideways. "I think we both recognize this conversation could become contentious so can we agree

in advance we're going to treat one another with respect, without resorting to name calling, and seek to understand one another as much as we seek to be understood? Maybe we could simply agree the Golden Rule is going to rule?" The advantage of using the Golden Rule is it is almost universally accepted and understood as "good." That makes it a good place from which to converse with people from a wide variety of worldviews.

- **Sharing your position.** You may be tempted to say "the Bible says" or "my church teaches," but those are authorities for you, not the person with whom you are conversing. So, speak the Truth, but make it your own. For example, "I have given this a lot of thought, and after serious consideration, I still believe the best formula for marriage is one man and one woman. To me, marriage is more than just a social partnership. It's something mysterious and holy. That's where I am— but you may see things differently. I'd really like to know where you are on this."

- **Being prepared to provide the basis of Truth on which you stand.** "As a Christian, I acknowledge that the Bible is God's Word. That means that what the Bible says has an authority that informs every area of my life. If you are interested, I could show you why I think this way."

- **Before parting ways, invite the continuation of the conversation** at another time over a shared meal. It can feel risky, but the worst someone can say is no. Table fellowship has a way of breaking down barriers talking on its own cannot. If appropriate, invite them for a meal at your home. There's a reason ambassadors move into the culture and set up a place to which people can come and learn the customs of another kingdom and be exposed to foreign ideas. Christ has a way of making Himself known in the breaking of bread.

One final thought: mom was right. If you can't say something nice you should seriously consider not saying anything at all. If you're feeling more like Jonah then Jesus, step away. People do not need more condemnation. They need transforming encounters with agents of God's grace and ambassadors of Christ's Kingdom.

QUESTIONS FOR PERSONAL REFLECTION AND GROUP DISCUSSION

1. What was your wake-up call to the concern of God for you and for others?
2. What did Betty's story about getting up in the dark help you see about how your own story can be woven with a passage of the Bible as the living Word?
3. How do the stories of Joseph, Daniel, and Paul inform the conversation about perspective on life from a worldly versus Kingdom point of view?
4. Who do you know that brings God into the room, the conversation or the situation simply by showing up?
5. What issues in the culture trigger your Jonah tendencies and how can you begin to see the person first and then together consider the issue with which they are dealing?

CHAPTER 8

Counteracting Fake Good News

Do you remember the advent of fake news? Taking advantage of the power of social media and playing on the distrust Americans have developed for one another and the mainstream media over the course of time, fake news trafficked in lies masquerading as truth. Not knowing what to believe or who to trust, Americans seemed willing to believe almost anything.

Students of the Bible are familiar with a character known as the father of lies. He trades in deception and he is the adversary of all that is authentically good, beautiful, and true. The father of lies perverts our thinking. It is his oldest tactic and once his hooks are set in a human mind, changing that mind requires liberation from literal shackles of sin and death. People, following the lie and the liar, become convinced that what God has called good is not good. They grow confused about human identity, Creation, sexuality, and morality. People are also deceived into exchanging the truth about God for lies and truth itself is perverted.

Christians, who know the Truth, follow the One who is the Truth, and have been set free by the Truth, find themselves declaring life in a culture of death, purity in a culture of debauchery, and truth in a culture convinced that truth is passé. The generation in which we live is actually labeled post-truth and fake news is a problem recognized by even those who say there is no absolute truth.

Christians are charged with representing Christ to *this* culture, here and now.

The Truth is:

- Not just any god, but God
- Not just any way to salvation, but Christ the only way
- Not just any words, but the Word of God

Why should anyone believe us? How do we establish trust, earn the right to be heard, and speak The Truth in a culture where the father of lies has so many operatives?

Trust is key. So, can people trust you? Can they trust you to tell the Truth, the whole truth, and nothing but the truth, so help you God? Can they trust you to be a person not only of your word but a person of The Word? And can you be trusted to keep it?

Beyond establishing trust, we also have to figure out how to gain a hearing. Our culture is abuzz with information, so how do we grab the attention of a selfie culture that wants to see and be seen? We put God on display. We become living demonstrations of the fullness of the Gospel in all its beauty and truth.

The good news is God is a bit of an exhibitionist—showing Himself in myriad ways all the time. God reveals Himself in creation, in the Scriptures of the Old and New Testaments, and in the person of Christ. Those who have eyes to see, see evidence of God all the time, everywhere. But many still live as if God is not. For them God sends the Church, empowered by His own Spirit, to shine as a light in the darkness—holding out the word of truth to the present generation. That is the Church's mission in the world.

But the father of lies has recruited a pantheon of colorful characters competing for the world's attention and affection. Contributing to the confusion is the cold hard fact that history is riddled with times and places in which God was openly mischaracterized and His Word so misrepresented that God was not only misunderstood but maligned. Jesus spoke millstone condemnation upon those who would so mislead people from the Truth, but we face the challenge of undoing what the faker's hath wrought.

Those half-truths and outright lies lead people to believe things which are not true and they become captive to the father of lies. They mistrust who God is, what He has done, what He wants and why He matters. The role of the Christian then is to confront and unmask the caricatures of God masquerading in the culture. And to replace them with living demonstrations of the fullness of the Gospel so the world may know who God really is.

Each generation faces its own set of imposters. If we imagine them as pageant contestants parading their ideas before us with the goal of attracting us to their way of thinking, then some of the competitors vying for attention and affection today are: Miss Nomer, Miss Information, Miss Characterization, Miss Understood, Miss Guided, Miss Directed, Miss Led, and the queen of the bunch, Miss Representation.

We will unmask each one and then talk about how to confront her lies with truth.

Miss Nomer

Miss Nomer enjoys playing word games with friends. She knows God has a name, but she finds pleasure in name-calling that reduces God to something less mysterious, less majestic, and less holy than He really is. Miss Nomer likes to nickname God with functions, attributes, metaphors, or names that leave open the possibility that God is a mere metaphor. So, where God reveals Himself to be love, Miss Nomer would have us think we possess the liberty to pervert that truth by saying that love is god.

Miss Nomer is not a new problem. She's been around a long time evidenced by the fact the Old Testament is replete with statements about God's concern for the use and misuse of His name. The third commandment says, "You shall not misuse the name of the Lord your God, for the Lord will not hold anyone guiltless who misuses his name" (Exodus 20:7). If God cares that much about His name, so should we.

In Leviticus 19:12 we have an instructive verse about the rightful use of God's name. It says, "Do not swear falsely by my name and so profane the name of your God. I am the Lord." Here we have a principle that is broadly applicable in our personal and public life. Think of all the places in our culture where you have heard God's name invoked. Have you thought about the fact those invocations of God's name are either honoring or profaning God's name?

When a person testifies in court, they take an oath to tell the truth, the whole truth, and nothing but the truth, so help them God—God's name is in play and God opposes perjury. When our civil servants take the oath of office with their hand on the Bible and conclude their oath with "so help me God," the name of God is invoked and that person has obligated themselves before God to keep their vows. The same holds true for vows of marriage and ordination. It is serious business to invoke the name of God in everything from the OMG on your text message to the GD of casual profanity. Miss Nomer has found her way into our daily parlance and we need to root her out. God takes His name seriously and so must we.

What does that look like in daily life? First, it is about being mindful. When you see it and when you hear it, make an actual mental note. Consider what you're thinking about and think about why that person or advertiser or media personality is using that particular expression. If you are with fellow believers or with kids, point it out. Take every opportunity to help others see what has become so much a part of the wallpaper of post-truth culture few even consciously notice. If you actually start looking for evidence of God's name taken in vain, you will see just how much of our culture has become profane. Even then, the real issue is not the name, but the reality of who God is. Taking His name in vain is merely a symptom of a deeper problem.

If God really is God then, as Frances Schaeffer said, "He is there and He is not silent."[1] The most basic truth a person must acknowledge before any conversation can be had about the issues we confront personally, in our families, in our country or in the world is the question of God's objective reality. If God is not objectively real then any further conversation about how we see things from a Biblical worldview is just foolishness.

On the other hand, if God is objectively real, and by grace, God really does make Himself known; that changes EVERYTHING. We are not alone. History is not without hope. Events are not meaningless. People are not without purpose. Evil does not triumph.

And we don't just know *of* God, we know God by name. That is amazing!

In a world obsessed with people seeking to make a name for themselves, Christians offer the gift of knowing not only the name above every name, but a relationship with the One who bears that name. That's better than Miss Nomer every day.

As with everything, we need to start with ourselves. Check your own use of OMG and its variants. When you catch yourself, confess, repent, and spend some time talking with God about God and godliness. We cannot escape the fact we're swimming in polluted waters, but we can spend intentional moments each day giving God His due in the midst of it. When the billboard or the bus wrap or the rapper or your social media feed uses God's name in any way short of His glory, just turn to Him and say, "Yes, Father, I see it. I heard it. I'm living with a moment by moment awareness of the world but my eyes are fixed on you." It only takes a moment, but in the moment you have honored God and kept yourself pure and undefiled by the world.

Miss Nomer is fairly easily vanquished by doing a combination of things. First, we have to know God personally so we can represent Him as He is to others. Second, we have to know people personally so we call them by name. Third, we need to introduce those we know to each other. Jesus came to make the Father known to us and sends us to make the two of them known to others. And by grace, the third member of the Trinity makes it possible for us to do just that. God is good. (But notably, although Miss Nomer might try to convince you otherwise, good is not god.)

Miss Information

In the part of the pageant where contestants answer questions to show how smart they are, Miss Information takes the stage. She asserts, "Intelligent people know the difference between myths and reality. Smart people don't believe in Santa Claus or the Easter Bunny or any other invisible supernatural. It's time people get with the times and leave all the fantasy savior narratives to comic books and religious nuts."

She's a smarty-pants who is too big for her britches. Miss Information trades in the currency of the contemporary intellect and she's more than happy to scorn any and all who aren't as well educated as she perceives herself to be. She's seeks to pit science against religion and reason against revelation. She too has old friends who make appearances in the Bible like the philosophers with whom Paul debated in Athens in Acts 17. She would like to see your neck stiffened and your heart hardened to the Word and the Spirit of God.

Scripture exposes Miss Information as one whose meta-narrative is designed to bring the Way of Truth into disrepute (2 Peter 2:2–3). Paul talks about her in Ephesians 4 as the source of "every wind of teaching" that is "cunning and crafty...deceitful scheming." It may be the wisdom of the world and it may seem like it puts us on the right side of history, but Miss Information will leave us on the utterly wrong side of the Holy God. Miss Information ought not be followed, but instead, called out, corrected, and invited into the Truth.

Miss Information is hard at work all around us and she's working in classrooms and textbooks and movies and media and, yes, new religious groups of secular humanists who want to adopt the forms without the faith because they crave meaning and community.

In my experience, Miss Information is one of the characters aligned against the Truth that only comes out by prayer. God has to change the heart and mind of the unbeliever so there will be receptivity to accurate information about who God is and what He has done. But that does not mean we do not contend directly with her in the public square or in private conversations.

Calling out Miss Information can be intimidating because we think she knows more than we do about a lot of things. But here's the truth: the Christian has the mind of Christ and He knows everything. He knows the mind of the person with whom you are speaking. He even knows what's behind what they're thinking. He's got this. Just let Him have you in the midst of it.

Second Corinthians 10:3–5 reminds us that although "we walk in the flesh, we are not waging war according to the flesh. For the weapons of our warfare are not of the flesh but have divine power to destroy strongholds. We destroy arguments and every lofty opinion raised against the knowledge of God, and take every thought captive to obey Christ." Miss Information doesn't stand a chance when confronted with the Truth.

Miss Characterization

Miss Characterization presents Christ as something other than He is and contrary to what the Bible reveals Him to be. Miss Characterization doesn't like that Jesus was incarnate as a physical man so she characterizes Him as Christa or a Christ essence. She doesn't like that He is revealed to be the eternally coexistent second member of the Trinity because she doesn't like the God revealed in the Old Testament. So, Miss Characterization presents Jesus as distinct and disconnected from the Father. But in contradiction to that, she also wants Jesus to serve her purposes if there is going to be some kind of cosmic reckoning before a holy God. So, she takes what the Bible says about Jesus being the only way to salvation and she extends that salvation to everyone. She prefers to imagine that no one will ever face eternal judgment so she does away with the idea that Jesus is coming again to judge the living and the dead. But to be honest, she doesn't really like the idea of the Truth of the Gospel at all and prefers to characterize Jesus as a Christ-figure. He wasn't actually the Christ because we don't really need one of those.

You can see her coming a mile away because she attracts a crowd with her scoffing at God's holiness. She makes God out to be a caricature of His True self. Miss Nomer feeds off of and feeds into Miss Characterization's antics.

Miss Characterization is a modalist, a redactionist, and a reductionist. One of her ploys is to separate God's revelation of Himself in the Old Testament from the New. She also likes to separate Jesus, the historical person, from the biblical witness to Jesus as the Word of God. She sees Jesus as good but much of the Bible as bad news. She wants you to have your best life now and use Jesus as you will, but without receiving Him as Savior or honoring Him as Lord.

She has advocates like the Yale professor Tom Krattenmaker whose book *Confessions of a Secular Jesus Follower* purports to evacuate Jesus from the religion of Christianity and make Him accessible as a guide for nonreligious people like himself. Touted as a "rediscovery of Jesus" this is really nothing more than co-opting Christ for one's own use. It makes of Jesus a caricature of His real self. A less-than Jesus who fits an individual's preferences.

Miss Characterization must be confronted. Yes, Jesus came as the Prince of Peace to give people the peace that passes all understanding, but that is contorted by humanists to mean Jesus teaches us how to build more self-centered peaceful lives. Nothing could be further from the truth. Jesus says of himself, "I came not to bring peace, but the sword." Miss Characterization does not appreciate when these particular details of Jesus' life and teaching are raised to the surface. She's seeking to actively suppress such inconvenient truths.

Yes, Jesus is a distinct person from God the Father and distinct from the Holy Spirit, but the three are One God, with one will being worked out in a redemptive plan of history over which they are utterly sovereign. While Jesus is the name above every name, He is, at the same time and always, the Alpha and the Omega, and the great I am. To characterize Him as anything less is a caricature.

To look in the mirror and make a Jesus in your own image captures the spirit of Miss Characterization. To vanquish her, we need to be conformed instead to the image of Christ, cultivate the mind of Christ on the matters of the day, and then speak The Truth of who He really is every time someone reduces Him to something less.

Miss Understood

Miss Understood is a little easier to handle. She's more a victim than a villain. We need to deal gently with such characters. She's more confused than committed to a cause.

You will find Miss Understood playing with words and ideas, venerating angels, seeking the blessing of animals, and dancing at full moon parties just because she was invited. She's a member of a church and reads Christian bloggers and she sees nothing wrong with participating in Mardi Gras, Sunday morning soccer leagues, or supplementing her faith experiences with alternative approaches to spirituality. She knows just enough Bible stories to be dangerous but she does not know the Bible nor its Author. She made a commitment to Jesus at a youth camp or women's conference or church confirmation course, she can't remember which. But that doesn't matter because she doesn't want to get too crazy about the whole thing. She's got spiritual friends who influence her more then she influences them. She's living in the real world, raising real kids, dealing with real issues. She thinks born-again Christian types are out to rob of her of her joy.

The points of entry into conversation with Miss Understood are literally myriad. But we must tread gently. She is easily offended and will more quickly defend her friend's non-Christian practices than the Christ she claims to follow. Grant her grace because in her heart of hearts she wants to be good and do good. She's honestly confused because she's been swimming in the cultural waters of feminism, self-promotion, self-fulfillment, and me-and-Jesus Christianity for a lifetime. She doesn't know what she doesn't know but she's interested.

The Christmas and Easter seasons are good points of entry for conversation because the culture has co-opted so many words and images that finding something to talk about is easy. Miss Understood has adopted her own version of many parts of the story and she knows the storyline of the Nutcracker better than she knows the actual accounts of Jesus' birth. Miss Understood is highly social, loves to include her kids, and doesn't want to be left out of anything, so invite her into an Advent or Lenten experience that you're doing with your kids.

Or just start by exploring one widely misunderstood aspect of the Christmas story. There were many more than three wise men from the East and they didn't show up until Jesus was nearly a year old. We think of three because three are named and three gifts given. But the kind of men we're talking about would have travelled with an entourage and a defense force. They would have come across the desert in what might have appeared to be a small invasion. Their visit would have constituted a geopolitical event for the Roman Empire.

Miss Understood will want very much to lighten the mood of the conversation so you should be prepared to talk about things like "Santa Claus is coming to town." Have you ever really thought about the lyrics to the most popular of all Christmas carols?

Consider the refrain and then ask yourself: Who sees our children when they're sleeping? Who knows when they're awake? Who knows when they've been bad or good and who gets to define those moral categories in your family? Is the threat of withholding material gifts really the motivation we want for our kids as to "why" they choose to do what's right? I'm not suggesting you never sing the song, I'm suggesting you have the conversation about how the qualities attributed to Santa are actually attributes of God.

God is the giver of every good and perfect gift.

God is the only one who sees and knows all things.

God is the one who defines what is good and therefore, what is bad.

God is keeping an account but Christmas is actually all about that account being paid in full by the greatest gift ever given—wrapped in human flesh and lying in a manger.

See how easy it is to help Miss Understood see what's she's been missing?

When my niece lost her first tooth my sister went with all the tooth fairy fun. But the jig was up before it really got started. My niece told me in no uncertain terms when she was six, "Auntie Carmen, don't tell Mom because it's really fun for her, but there is no tooth fairy." Having had a similar conversation with her when she was four about the baby Jesus, I knew arguing was futile. "You seem pretty certain so how do you know?"

"Mommy and Daddy love us too much to let someone sneak around in our house at night. No way they're letting someone into my room. So there's no tooth fairy."

By the same logic there's no Santa and no Elf on the Shelf. Kids know, and when we persist in lying to the ones who figure it out we compound the confusion.

Miss Understood is a follower and she's easily moved by the cultural currents of the day. She has believed Miss Information, adapted her vocabulary to Miss Nomer, and adopted less-than-Jesus notions from Miss Characterization. Intervention is essential. She is only proceeding down a path of half-truths because no one has stopped and invited her to think about what she's thinking about.

We cannot lead people to truth by half-truths. So, where we know Miss Understood exists, it is incumbent upon us to gently offer guidance. Which leads us to twins in our pageant, Miss Guided and Miss Directed.

Miss Guided and Miss Directed (and their disciple, Miss Led)

These twins are quite popular in the culture today and they have many followers. They set a course by a moral compass keyed to the desires of the hearts and they lead people down a wide path to destruction. But they're so fun to be with their followers fail to ask about the dead end toward which they're being misled.

Miss Guided and Miss Directed operate by what is often referred to as the spirit of the age. Every age has one. It is a set of cultural influences, ideas, events, and movements when taken together can be described as a spirit of the day. It is the consensus opinion, the cultural current, what some call the arc of history, and it almost always bends toward liberalism. Miss Guided and Miss Directed are its ambassadors who make it all look, feel, and sound acceptable as society gradually drifts further from what is objectively good, noble, beautiful, and true.

1. The Psalmist calls it walking in the counsel of the wicked (Psalm 1).
2. Paul called it walking in the "course of this world" (Ephesians 2:1-2).
3. Solomon called it the path where fools rush in (Proverbs 1:15).
4. Jesus called it the wide gate and broad road that leads to destruction (Matthew 7:13).

By whatever description, Miss Guided and Miss Directed are leading people blithely toward a dead end via a system of ideas and values that result in a lifestyle at enmity with God.

The generation that follows Miss Guided and Miss Directed is Miss Led.

The antidote is Wisdom and God alone knows the way to it. Indeed, the Holy Spirit is the Guide we need to lead us in paths of righteousness. He gives us the counsel we need to live in the world, but not become of it.

With the Spirit of God guiding us into all truth, we are positioned to help direct and lead others in the Way of righteousness. It's a narrow way, but every other path leads to destruction.

Miss Representation

I've saved the nastiest for last. Miss Representation is not what she appears to be and she is not what she purports to be. She's a wolf in sheep's clothing. She is the counterfeit Christian leader about whom we have been warned: "there will be false teachers among you, who will secretly bring in destructive heresies, even denying the Master who bought them" (excerpt from II Peter 2:1). Jude 1:4 offers a similar warning, "For certain people have crept in unnoticed...ungodly people, who pervert the grace of our God into sensuality and deny our only Master and Lord, Jesus Christ." This is a description of Miss Representation.

Miss Representation is a false teacher who uses the world to woo, satiate, stupefy, and entertain people down paths of destruction that ultimately lead to death. She is the one about whom Jesus warned you (John 10:10), but she doesn't look like the devil you've come to expect. She is the spirit of the world Paul describes as having worked its way into the church (I Corinthians 2:12) and we've become so comfortable having her around we've unwittingly accepted many of her lies as truth.

And lest you think this migration from truth is occurring on its own, it is time to wake up to the reality of the intentional efforts of those who possess a secular or humanistic worldview. While it is accurate to say cultures drift over time, American culture is being systematically and intentionally reoriented away from God. The humanists have an agenda and a plan and they are working their plan with great effectiveness. Their goal is to delegitimize God and humiliate those who believe in Him, undermine every religiously affiliated institution, and make Christians feel the fool in every conversation.

The game-plan to reorient the American mind and culture away from God includes efforts within the arenas of the media, the courts, government, academia, and the church. But the real battle is being waged in the mind of each person we know and love. Our parents, our kids, our friends, our colleagues, our neighbors, and our spouses are under continual assault and it is easy to follow after the beauties of Miss

Nomer, Miss Information, Miss Characterization, Miss Understood, Miss Guided, and Miss Directed, and become Miss Led.

We have to recognize the reality and then we have to accurately represent the name, character, and Spirit of God by providing truthful information people can understand. We have to guide and direct people into all Truth.

What do we do when we meet them on the street?

So, what do we do when we meet Miss Nomer, Miss Information, Miss Characterization, Miss Understood, Miss Guided, Miss Directed, Miss Led, or Miss Representation on the street or in the sanctuary? We follow the counsel of Scripture to

- Recall truth
- Recognize falsehood
- Reinforce reliance upon God
- Reach out in truth, no matter what

We remain faithful, fruitful, and we persevere.
Jude 17–23 says:

> But you must *remember*, beloved, the predictions of the apostles of our Lord Jesus Christ. They said to you, "In the last time there will be scoffers, following their own ungodly passions." It is these who cause divisions, worldly people, devoid of the Spirit. But you, beloved, *building yourselves* up in your most holy faith and praying in the Holy Spirit, *keep yourselves* in the love of God, *waiting* for the mercy of our Lord Jesus Christ that leads to eternal life. And *have mercy* on those who doubt; *save others* by snatching them out of the fire; *to others show mercy with*

fear, hating even the garment stained by the flesh. (Emphasis added)

Jude tells us to remember the apostles' teachings. Recall the truth and rely upon it. Then he tells us to recognize falsehood: scoffers who are following their own ungodly passions. You recognize them because they cause division in the Body of Christ, they are worldly people and the Spirit who lives within you recognizes no bond of peace with the spirit of the world in them. Then it's time to reinforce our reliance upon God. Faced with the reality of false teaching and false teachers, we need to be built up in faith, prayed up in the Spirit, upheld by the love of God, and filled with mercy—not anger.

The people who are held hostage by Miss Information, Miss Characterization, Miss Directed, Miss Representation and the like, are not bad people. They're more like prisoners of war than actual conscious combatants for the Enemy. Most of them have never actually thought about what they're thinking about and their "thinkin' is stinkin'," to quote my husband.

In the same way Jesus has compassion on all of us who were once slaves to sin, we must have compassionate concern for those following after false teachers. They do not know their guides are blind. They do not know they are being led down a path of destruction.

And yes, that means we can't turn tail and run when this litany of worldly pageant participants comes at us on the runways of life. Miss Representation and her pals have to be confronted, corrected, and certainly called out. Jude characterizes it as staying close enough to the false teaching that some might be snatched out of the fire of their destructive ideas. And how are people attracted away from the often mesmerizing flames? By the truth of the Gospel and the excellence of our lives. Yes, we stand at all times ready to offer a defense for the hope in us, but we also simply live such good lives among the pagans that when the world sees us—even as we are maligned by its leaders—people actually see the fruit of love among us and are drawn away from darkness to light.

QUESTIONS FOR PERSONAL REFLECTION AND GROUP DISCUSSION

1. Which of the Misses in this chapter are most attractive to you and why?
2. Share a time in your life when you followed Miss Guided or Miss Led down a path from which you ultimately had to repent.
3. Can you identify a time when you were drawn in and fell for Miss Representation or Miss Information? How did you eventually sort out the truth from the lies?
4. People can become thoroughly convinced by these imposters and construct an entire worldview around a lie. What is the starting point of conversation with a person who is wholly committed to an unholy and false cosmology?

CHAPTER 9

Offering a Reorientation to Truth Consistent with Reality

When we look around and see and hear and feel the sadness, stress, loneliness, brokenness, pain, and despair of the world, we know in the depths of our beings this is not the way it's supposed to be. But most people, and many Christians, are actually in the dark when it comes to knowing how it is supposed to be.

God knows we're in the dark. It's an age-old problem to which God has—and is—the solution. God is light.

Light and dark are persistent characters throughout the Bible. They make their first appearance in Genesis 1 and by the end of the drama, only light remains.

Take the time to read the following passages where you will see the juxtaposition of light and darkness throughout the full scope of redemptive history:

- Genesis chapter 1
- The Gospel of John chapter 1
- Colossians chapter 1
- First John chapter 1
- Revelation chapters 21–22

In the Beginning, before He created anything that is seen, God made seeing possible by the creation of light. The very idea that light had to be called forth and spoken into reality gives an indication of just how dark darkness can be. Quite literally, without light, we cannot see. By God's creative genius He gives us the physical reality of light to also illuminate a deep spiritual truth: without the Light, we cannot see.

Most people living today are spiritually blind. They lack awareness of the Light by which to accurately see God, themselves, and the world around them. Into the darkness of their present disorientation and desperation, we shine as those who bear the good news of the Light of the Gospel.

If you've ever been in a very dark room for a very long time you know how painful and even frightening it can be for the light to suddenly shine. We must keep this in mind as we enter conversations with others. Again, we turn to Jesus for instruction.

In the Gospel of John, chapter 3, there is a well-known verse of Scripture: "For God so loved the world, that He gave His only Son, that whoever believes in Him should not perish but have eternal life" (John 3:16).

But verse 16 does not appear in a vacuum. It appears in the context of a paragraph, in the context of a chapter about old and new life, in the context of the book of John's gospel, in the context of the Bible, in the context of God's creative and redemptive plan. And the characters of light and dark make a notable appearance as light comes to life and darkness meets its nemesis who will finally and utterly destroy it.

Verse 16 leads off a paragraph which goes on to read:

> For God so loved the world, that He gave His only Son, that whoever believes in Him should not perish but have eternal life. For God did not send His Son into the world to condemn the world, but in order that the world might be saved through him. Whoever believes in Him is not condemned, but whoever does not believe is condemned already, because he has not believed in the name of the only Son of God. And this is the judgment: *the light* has come into the world, and people loved *the darkness* rather than *the light* because their works were evil. For everyone who does wicked things hates *the light* and does not come to *the light*, lest his works should be exposed. But whoever does what is true comes to *the light*, so that it may be clearly seen that his works have been carried out in God. (Emphasis added)

These words of Jesus make clear God knows once we are aware of the light, we become aware of the darkness. That is a moment of truth. At that moment, and in every subsequent moment, we choose: the darkness or the light? The father of lies or the Truth? The way of destruction or the Way and the Life? We cannot have it both ways and Jesus is the dividing line. Judgmental? Yes, read the passage again. This is judgment, articulated by the Judge. Those who would set themselves in judgment over Him are not only in darkness, they are agents of it.

The best Christmas gift I think I've ever received serves now as a bookmark in my Bible. The child who gave it to me said, "Lots of people ignore the light of the world." He looked at the card which he was fingering and when he looked up at me his brow was furrowed. He repeated his concern, "Lots of people ignore the light of the world." But this time he added with deep seriousness, "Don't." With that he handed me the homemade treasure: an index card with bright yellow dot he colored. It is a reminder to me of the Light of the world and the great responsibility to not ignore Him.

Darkness is real and for many, darkness is preferred to light. An anonymous pre-Christian Greek proverb says, "We can easily forgive a child who is afraid of the dark; the real tragedy is when men are afraid of the light." This philosopher is not operating out of a Christian worldview, but his observation bears witness to the reality of God's general revelation in creation itself.

Reality was darkness until God created light (Genesis 1). God is light and gave His Word to be a lamp for the feet and a light to the path of His people (Psalm 119:105). But the reality of humanity was darkness until God the Father sent Jesus the Son to be the light of the world (John 1:1–13). In Jesus Christ, light dawned (Matthew 4:16). During His earthly life, Jesus' light opened blind eyes, illuminated darkened hearts, and penetrated the shadowy places. Indeed, He is the light of the world (John 8:12).

Upon His death, resurrection, and ascension into heaven, the Holy Spirit ignites the light within believers and empowers them to be the light of the world (Matthew 5:14–16). We, who walk in the light of God's redemption, are now the light of the world. We are sent to let our light so shine before others they will see our good works and glorify God. Indeed, we are "a chosen people, a royal priesthood, a holy nation, a people belonging to God, that we may declare the praises of Him who called us out of darkness into His wonderful light" (I Peter 2:9).

We have known darkness and now, by God's grace, we know light and the lightness of being. But the darkness persists and many of our neighbors continue to live without a knowledge of the light. That's where we come in. We are now charged with walking into the darkness with the light of Christ by the same Spirit with whom Jesus left the glory of Heaven and took on all the darkness of human reality so we might be redeemed. That's how much He loves us and that is how much He calls us to love others.

If we began to see our neighbors not as bad people, but as people who are born into, raised, and living in deep darkness, our hearts would break at the fear, dread, and hopelessness they are experiencing. Imagine if darkness were all you ever knew?

Darkness is disorienting. In the darkness of depression, depravity, abuse, fatigue, need, and loneliness, people will grasp at anything for comfort, meaning, and hope. When the Church and her people are not there to bear witness to the reality of God's goodness, beauty, and truth, the Enemy will fill hands and hearts and minds and lives with lesser things.

Throughout history, individuals with a variety of ideologies have set themselves up in opposition to the revealed reality of God. They make "truth" claims over and against the Truth. They construct cosmologies devoid of God or at least avoiding God. Some are more organized than others and some have status as competing religions. For twenty-first-century Americans the ideology growing in popularity is that of humanism.

Humanism has grown out of a confluence of ideas in the early 1940s and today includes 25 percent of the American population who are unaffiliated with any recognizable religion. Known as secularists, secular humanists, humanists, and atheists, adherents are challenged to transition from that which has historically been an intellectual philosophy to an actual social movement. Part of the challenge is when they lay claim to truth or moral superiority, or declare that a certain set of values should be universally applied, building cohesion is difficult because there is no objective basis upon which to stake their claim. Morality is whatever the majority determines to be moral if there is no objective moral standard.

Humanists want fellowship, just without faith. They want the sense of community without the unity of the Spirit or the bond of peace that comes from Christ. They declare themselves right without righteousness and they are, in Biblical lingo, blind guides. People operating from a worldly perspective do not see that. Which is precisely the point.

Physical and spiritual darkness are both real. So too are physical and spiritual light. Part of the challenge we face is the co-opting of that language by The Enlightenment. Following the notable Dark Ages, the Age of Reason arose. We know it now as The Enlightenment. By that we mean an intellectual movement in Western Europe in the late seventeenth and eighteenth centuries that emphasized reason over revelation and individualism over tradition. It was (and we are today) heavily influenced by philosophers including Descartes, Locke, and Newton. Their ideas became the foundations of Kant, Goethe, Voltaire, Rousseau, and Adam Smith—and their ideas, in turn, form the foundations of most of our systems today. Most people now think what they think and think how they think because of this handful of Enlightenment-era philosophers.

The problem is the light of the moral philosophers in the group (Kant, Voltaire, and Rousseau) was the light of reason, not revelation. They advanced a set of ideas evident in the thinking of most of our neighbors today. That worldview says,

- Science-based education is the gateway to personal, societal, and global solutions
- Individuals determine their own identity and destiny

- Meaning is derived from what we do, build, achieve, accumulate, or create

Each of those claims is, at best, a half-truth. Science and technology are wonderful tools, but terrible masters. Our core identity is not something we create, but with which we are endowed. The idea that someone could have a personal destiny devoid of a personal beginning is delusional and meaning tied to achievement of any sort results in a utilitarian pragmatism that wipes out anyone who someone else does not see as useful.

You can see how we end up with abortion-on-demand for any reason, assisted suicide, and debates about the ethics of artificial intelligence or engineering organoids and human/animal hybrids in labs that are fully developed parts of people without actually being people.

The Enlightenment, and therefore humanism, does not and cannot answer the big questions of where we come from, why we're here, or what happens to us when we die. The Enlightenment holds at the same time an utterly impersonal view of reality while advocating the individual person as paramount. People don't see that because they only know what they've been taught and what they've been taught for the past three hundred years is Enlightenment philosophy.

The Christian stands in the unique position of being able to shed light on The Enlightenment. We know the real Light of life and we know it's a person, not an idea. In the final analysis, the Gospel is the only credible explanation of reality.

Now, when we say *The Gospel* we mean more than "the Romans road" which is a popular track explaining the plan of salvation using passages from the book of Romans. The Gospel is in fact a comprehensive explanation of all of life. It explains our dilemma, evil in the world, natural disasters, and our need for something more than "this" by explaining who God is, God's redemptive plan for all things, here and forevermore.

We must not reduce the Gospel to anything less than its comprehensive nature. People living in deep darkness need the fullness of the Light of Christ, nothing less.

The darkness is dark and sometimes when we look at the world we are tempted to despair. Instead, let us see those places, people, and circumstances as opportunities for the Church to bear the reorienting Light of God's goodness and grace.

When you consider the world, what breaks your heart?

- Foster-care and the need for adoption
- Incarceration and the need for redemptive rehabilitation
- Human trafficking and the need for liberation from modern-day slavery
- The real war on women in the world and the need to end gendercide, female genital mutilation, and the practice of marrying off children as brides
- Abject poverty and the need for a restoration of dignity through education and an opportunity to work
- Neglect and abuse of the disabled and elderly and the need for a pro-life ethic for all life
- Systemic racism and the need for real reconciliation

These are not problems governments are going to solve. These are problems rooted in the darkness of human depravity. They only come out by prayer and the piercing of the heart by the Light of God. Some choose to critique, criticize, or vilify from the sidelines. The Christian's calling is to creatively confront, provide solutions the world would never dream of, and stand when all others shrink back in fear.

This is not just about making a difference, it's about making the world different—in a particular direction.

Here, we must talk about race. Conversations in America about the Confederate flag and Confederate monuments, the rise of white nationalism, and the race-based fear of our neighbors are conversations we must have. These conversations are difficult, complicated, and critical. Put simply, racism is contrary to the Gospel. So, what do we do with the realities of personal implicit bias and residual consequences of racism over generations? The first step is to admit that we have a problem and start talking with others instead of about them.

Then we must examine ourselves. As a Christian, do I recognize and celebrate the reality that I have brothers and sisters in Christ from every tribe and tongue? Do I amplify the light God is shining on this issue right now through my conversations? Does my heart on the matter of race reflect the truth that every human being is endowed with certain inalienable rights and deserves to be treated with dignity because they are an image bearer of God?

Getting to a righteous place on race starts with rightly understanding the Word of God and then rightly applying God's Word to the realities of life today.

Letting God's Word speak for itself, let's turn to the book of Philemon.

Paul was a member of the intellectual elite; Philemon was a wealthy Greek; Onesimus was a slave. They were separated racially, socioeconomically, and educationally. They had every superficial reason for racial prejudice, economic envy, and hatred. Yet the reality of their relationship could not be more radically different. Paul says of Onesimus the slave, "he is my very heart." He calls Philemon the Greek "beloved brother." There is a profound spiritual reality behind these substantially restored relationships and that is the message of the book of Philemon.

This short letter is a window into the beauty the Gospel brings to personal relationships.

While in prison, Paul met Onesimus who ran away from his master Philemon, one of Paul's converts in the church of Colossae. There in prison, Onesimus embraced the Gospel and was saved. Paul wrote this letter to Philemon on behalf of Onesimus, whom he was sending back to Philemon. Paul's manner is the epitome of gentleness and grace.

Though he affirms he could command Philemon, he rather appeals to him on the basis of love, verses 8–9. The substance of the appeal is that Philemon welcomes Onesimus no longer as a slave but as a beloved brother. "Welcome him as you would me," Paul says. There is complete confidence on the part of Paul that his appeal will be received and carried out. In fact Paul expects Philemon will do even more. "I know that you will do even more than I say." His expectation is based upon the transformational power of the Gospel and the personal intimate knowledge of his brother in Christ, Philemon, whom Paul knows will rightly submit to Paul's spiritual authority.

The Gospel not only answers the question "what is wrong with man?" It also provides the cure. You and I are not the product of an impersonal, time-plus-material-plus-chance origin. We are the intentional creation of a purposeful, willful, loving, holy, and personal-infinite God. The loss of fellowship we experience with God and the resulting loss of peace with others and ourselves is our fault, not God's. We chose (and we choose) to act in rebellion against the Creator and we lost our place—our right relationship—with Him. This affects our understanding of God, others, and ourselves. We are collectively and individually confused about issues of identity, work, governance, authority, purpose, and ultimate reality. The result is corruption, substitution, and temporal answers to eternal questions. There are longings within us nothing in this world can satisfy. In our dilemma we often accept incomplete or erroneous answers that lead not to life but to destruction.

The good news Paul spoke to Onesimus as a runaway slave is the same good news Paul declared to privileged Philemon. Both were slaves to sin, both were lost and both received the grace of God in Jesus Christ—through which they were not only substantially restored in relationship with God, they also came to see we stand with all other men on equal footing before the Cross. Onesimus and Philemon stood as forgiven men, redeemed and free.

The man who has experienced the forgiveness of his true moral guilt before God has been restored to a living personal relationship with his Creator. He has clarity concerning his true identity as a man made in the image of God. He has value and purpose. He is no longer lost and confused. He is also restored to the possibility of substantially transformed relationships with his fellow man. The ground beneath the cross is level. The precious blood of Christ shed there for me was also shed for my fellow man. Since God has loved him; I too must love Him. It does not matter that he be black or white. It does not matter that he be slave or free. It does not matter that he be intellectually superior or inferior. It does not matter that he be rich or poor. It does not matter that he be citizen or alien. He has value. He is precious. He is a person made in the image of God. God has loved that person. How can I not also love him? How much more if he too has bowed at the foot of the cross, confessed his sin, and been born again? He is then even more than my fellow man, he is my brother. We have experienced the same love and share the same hope. We share the same inheritance and the same eternal home. Neither of us are yet perfect, but we can offer to each other what we have experienced in Christ: redemptive love, restorative acceptance, and complete forgiveness.

The material humanist who believes human beings are merely the conjured result of time and chance has no basis for genuinely loving his fellow man. For that matter, he has no basis to even substantiate that *love* is real. If man is, after all, only highly organized socially conditioned matter, a mere product of chemical processes, the result of time and chance, what real value does he have? If the fittest survive why not eliminate all others who are just taking up space and using up valuable resources?

Follow the logic of the material-plus-time-plus-chance view of our existence to its logical conclusion and you arrive naturally at the conclusions of Adolf Hitler. Hitler is not wrong if the theory of evolution is right. Hitler believed the Arians were the master race. His thinking was based upon the theory of evolution. We consider his actions to be "atrocities" but why? Hitler's actions were simply the logical outcome of his having been taught the lie of material-plus-time-plus-chance philosophy in lieu of the Gospel.

The Gospel is the truth about reality. People are precious because they are created in the image of God. People are broken because they stand in rebellion against God. They suppress and exchange the truth of their personal beginning for the lie of secular humanism. The results are catastrophic.

People can be restored to a living relationship with their Creator and with each other based upon the reconciling work of Jesus Christ on the cross of Calvary. The blood He shed there is God's final statement on the value He places upon the individual. If God so loved—we also should so love—this stands alone as the only basis for good will among men.

Peace on earth and good will among men is only possible when the Prince of Peace reigns in the hearts of men. No lesser law will prevail against our wanton rebellion. Paul knew this and so appealed to the converted man, Philemon, to receive anew his brother in Christ, Onesimus—not under Paul's human apostolic authority, but in submission to Christ who alone is Lord of all.

What is required is not only a changed perspective but new eyes through which we see the world and those within it. We don't just need a heart transplant so we love God rightly, we need a mind transplant so we process what we see as God sees it.

The moment we lose sight of another person's humanity we have a problem. God sees people as real persons, created in His image, to the praise of His glory. As soon as we see people as anything less, we run afoul of the Biblical worldview. People are not a problem to be solved, a population to be controlled, a labor force to be exploited, a means of production to be managed, nor a mass to be manipulated. We are people. Red, yellow, black, and white, equally precious in God's sight.

But since the earliest days of humanity, we have not seen it that way. It seems we have never outgrown the Edenic urge of our first parents to be like God, or even to be god. Unsatisfied with God's perfect provision, we reach for more than we need. Unsatisfied with managing and stewarding that over which God has given us limited sovereignty, we have chosen to harm the Earth and subjugate one another. Failing to properly acknowledge the Lordship of God, we are obsessed with lording power and position over one another. The list goes on and we find ourselves in a place called the United States of America with a history with native peoples of which we are not proud and a history with enslaved African people of which we are greatly ashamed.

What then are we to do? Face the facts as people of faith. Not denying sin but confessing it. Declaring intrinsic equality, stepping out as ministers of reconciliation, eradicating injustice wherever it may be found, and ennobling others to live with the dignity and mutual respect of people created in the image of the living God.

God has provided all we need not only to confront racism in our society but the scourge of man's inhumanity to man in every other place and circumstance. Philemon is *The Gospel* applied to human relationships. So why is a nation where so many people have full and free access to the Word of God, where the Gospel is freely preached, so utterly corrupt?

While the Christian asks this question, the secular humanist asks the corollary, "if we are genuinely progressing socially and evolving physically then why do all the -isms that hinder our progress persist?" Together we respond with anemic acts of war, legislation, or regulation, attempting to rein in the sin that runs rampant. In fact, it reigns in many human hearts. We should all know by now government cannot govern a heart nor limit the lawlessness of a person or group that has determined to live in anarchy. And so, over and over again it happens. We may have outlawed slavery but racism persists. We may not commit infanticide like the Romans, but we have killed tens of millions of American children through abortion. We may know love is better than hate and yet radical jihadists want to drive the Saturday people (Jews) into the sea, followed by the Sunday people (Christians). Why?

Indeed, why. Why are humans so inhumane? An honest observer must conclude there is something intrinsically wrong with humanity. Something is wrong on the inside. People don't think, feel, nor act rightly. There is confusion and corruption concerning our very nature, our purpose, and even our personhood. The sexual perversity and confusion in our culture is one unavoidable example but it is only one among a host of evidence of our deep depravity.

James observes, "each one is tempted when, by his own evil desire, he is dragged away and enticed. Then, after desire has conceived, it gives birth to sin; and sin, when it is full-grown, gives birth to death." Ideas have consequences. They take root in our minds and they work themselves out in our attitudes and actions. Sin of thought becomes sin of affect, attitude, and articulation, and final action. Some ideas lead down paths of righteousness while others lead to death. Jesus said the first path is narrow and the second wide.

Knowing the Truth which sets men free, it becomes the responsibility of the Christian to illuminate the Way of Truth that leads to Life.

Truth is that which is consistent with reality but Truth is not a set of ideas learned from a book. Truth is a reorientation to reality that comes through a relationship with a person. So, let's get personal.

QUESTIONS FOR PERSONAL REFLECTION AND GROUP DISCUSSION

1. When you consider John 3:16 in the context of the paragraph where it appears, do you see it differently? If so, how so?
2. When you imagine trying to live in total darkness, how does it change your appreciation for the reality and gift of light?
3. Why is secular Humanism insufficient to provide a basis for morality and meaning?
4. When you consider the world and the various plights of people today, what breaks your heart?
5. How did the study of Philemon inform your perspective on racial reconciliation?

_____

_____

_____

_____

_____

_____

_____

_____

_____

_____

_____

_____

_____

CHAPTER 10

Getting God Back into Every Conversation by Reconnecting the Eternal with the Everyday

O pen any digital news source or any newspaper and the headlines will supply fodder for worldview conversations.

The front page is replete with wars and rumors of wars and politics that are national, local, and personal. There are issues related to science, technology, healthcare, education, entertainment, politics, sex, drugs, violence, racial division, and yes, sometimes overt stories about religion. As Bob Smietana once told me, "Every story has a religion angle, you just have to know where to look."

So, look at the Op-Ed, Science, Lifestyle, Obituaries, Comics, Sports, and Personals and bring the Christian worldview to bear on what people are saying, how events are described, how things are characterized. We can talk about anything with relevance and truth because God is real and relevant and true.

We practically get God back into *every* conversation by being fishers of men and finding the right hook. There's a reason they call fishermen anglers. So, where's the angle that reconnects the miraculous to the mundane and the eternal with the everyday?

Here's how it's done:

Take any headline and look for references to eternal, holy, supernatural realities.

Are there echoes of Biblical themes?

Are there allusions to Biblical stories people have forgotten are from the Bible?

Is there a Good Samaritan, someone reading the writing on the wall, or a pop star singing "Hallelujah?"

Is an athlete making the sign of the cross or pointing heavenward?

Is there a life or death question being asked, justice being weighed, or a moral boundary being crossed?

Look for the truth angle, the life angle, the identity angle, the Sin angle, the sovereignty angle, the justice angle, or the echo effect from the Bible people are missing.

All you do is point it out. In my experience, simply making the connection is enough to get the conversation going.

Jesus was the ultimate angler when it came to hooking people with Kingdom curiosity. What can we learn from His approach as we fish for men today?

Jesus was willing to talk to anyone, anytime, anywhere. He treated no one as an interruption and no subject as off-limits. He regarded each person as a person and each encounter as a divine appointment. He quite literally reconnected the eternal with the everyday through Himself, but also through what He said about the issues real people were confronting.

We could start anywhere with any one of Jesus' conversations. So, let's start with the well-known but often misunderstood woman at the well in the Gospel of John, chapter 4. You'll notice Jesus was on His way to Galilee and the shortest route was through Samaria. Jesus and all his disciples at the time were Jews. And the text clearly notes "Jews had nothing to do with Samaritans." Men also had nothing to do with women in the cultural context. But there's Jesus, starting a conversation with a woman at a well near the Samaritan town of Sychar. He's sent the disciples to run an errand so He's got time to talk.

The woman is interested in debating issues of religion and politics. Jesus is interested in her. That's a lesson for us. The other lesson for us here is Jesus doesn't see her the way the world sees her. And after her transforming encounter with Jesus, she has a whole new sense of herself.

Grace sat across the lunch table and just said, "Everyone I know is living to protect their wound. The wounds are different and some of them don't even remember how or when or who hurt them, but they're all living to protect their wound."

I thought about that for a moment. Is she right? Was the woman at the well there at midday to protect herself from the wound of shame from the other women who retrieved their water in the morning? Are people avoiding one another out of fear of being too fully known, found out, and further wounded for their transgressions? Jesus intentionally went through Samaria when He could have gone around it. Jesus also crossed over to the other side when He could have stayed put with the adoring crowds.

In Mark 4:35–41 we read:

> On that day, when evening had come, he said to them, "Let us go across to the other side." And leaving the crowd, they took him with them in the boat, just as he was. And other

boats were with him. And a great windstorm arose, and the waves were breaking into the boat, so that the boat was already filling. But he was in the stern, asleep on the cushion. And they woke him and said to him, "Teacher, do you not care that we are perishing?" And he awoke and rebuked the wind and said to the sea, "Peace! Be still!" And the wind ceased, and there was a great calm. He said to them, "Why are you so afraid? Have you still no faith?" And they were filled with great fear and said to one another, "Who then is this, that even the wind and the sea obey him?"

Again, Jesus is on the move. He is leading the disciples to cross over to the other side. In this case it's the other side of the sea of Galilee but it could have been leading them to cross over to the other side of town or cross over to the other side of whatever divides people. Note it's a bit of a flotilla. Yes, Jesus is in the boat with disciples but other boats are traveling with them. Everyone was subject to the sudden violent storm. The potential loss of life was great. The people were justifiably scared to death. And they did what we'd all do, they cried out to Jesus!

Note when they wake Jesus He deals first with the cause of their fear and then He deals with them. There's a lesson there for us. People cannot hear the words of correction until the wound is healed, the hunger satisfied, the cause of the fear quelled.

When Jesus entered a conversation, the conversation changed. Every time. I can imagine there were lots of occasions when people said, "What were we talking about before He got here?" And others would respond, "I can't remember." Because what they were talking about after the fact was Jesus.

Jesus spoke with people, He didn't speak to issues. Why is that? Because for Jesus the issue is always the same: the issue is redemption. We can learn a lot from the way He reframed conversations to help others see the supernatural and eternal perspective on temporal realities. How can we do that in our everyday conversations?

Again, let's look to see how the first disciples did it. We're not Jesus, but as disciples filled with the same Spirit we have a hope to offer others no one else on earth can give them. God has set divine appointments for us to keep everyday on His behalf. We just have to be open to the possibility.

The issue is the sexual revolution and emerging generations

Liza is eleven. She is privileged by every definition of that term. She has a strong Christian generational lineage. Her great grandmother, who died the year Liza was born, was as godly a woman as I have ever known. Her daughters are likewise wise women of virtue and grace. Their children, who are my age, range from faith-keepers to boundary testers to utterly culturally accommodating church-goers. Liza knows no need and lacks no access to the world of technology. She is a consumer of the culture and her mother now recognizes just how toxic a diet her daughter has been ingesting.

The conversation was about romantic love and Liza's mom was dutifully explaining the nature of things. She started, "When a man and woman fall in love—" when Liza interrupted, "or two people of the same sex." The mom looks at me and says, "I realized all at once that my child had been educated to believe something that I don't believe but I also realized that I wasn't actually sure how to respond. I asked her who told her that and she said, 'Mom, it's just a preference.'"

Okay, deep breath. As is true for every generation, our kids are growing up in a world very different from the one in which we were raised. Technology and social media mean our kids are dealing with pornography and varieties of peer pressure and cyber-bullying that are new varieties of old problems. They are also being led by the overwhelming majority of cultural influencers to believe gender is fluid and there is no such thing as sexual deviancy. It's not even a question of whether or not it feels good, culture says that even if it hurts and you want to do it, do it. Self-harming and moral questions related to sexuality are conversations for which every one of us must be equipped.

To Liza we say, "Honey, you are absolutely right, it is a matter of preference, but not in the way you think. The preference belongs to God. God made people in His image. We're not angels and we're not animals, we're human beings. That makes us totally unique in all of Creation. How many times have you been told you're unique, precious, and one of a kind?" If Liza is honest, the answer is "lots of times." So ask her, "What makes you, you?"

She is likely to answer with a combination of what can be categorized as nature (biology, personality, immutable traits, and characteristics) and nurture (relationships, roles, activities, privileges). We then help her see those two categories explaining, "That is all true, but none of those descriptions tells the whole truth of who you are or who God created you to be. You would not be here at all if mommy and daddy preferred not to follow God's preference for shared love in creating you. You are the particular twenty-three sets of chromosomes and have the ancestors you have and you are who you are as a daughter, granddaughter, sister, and friend, because mommy and daddy are who we are and did not follow the world's thinking on romantic love as a momentary preference. I believe what God says when He tells us we are created in His image, male and female. Somehow, in a way only known to God, that reflects who God is. That's the way God prefers it and I prefer to follow His lead."

From Liza who's eleven, let's move to Robert who was fifteen and a freshman in high school when the following encounter took place. He's always been an artistic, joyful person. He's bright and friendly and handsome. He was being pursued by a boy who was on both his swim team and in drama. The problem? Robert likes girls and he didn't like the attention he was receiving from this aggressive gay boy. Robert attends an elite prep school with a Christian heritage but no expressly Christian moral code for students. I was visiting with his mom one day and he lingered in the kitchen longer than usual. I could tell he was looking for an opportunity to talk.

"Robert, what's the greatest challenge you're facing at school?" I inquired, offering an open-ended question he could keep on the surface or take as deep as he wanted.

"School's good," he said and then I allowed time to pass sensing we were in the midst of a long pause in a sentence and then gently nudged. "School's good—so what's bad?" I asked.

He looked over at me without really lifting his head from the food on the counter, his brow was furrowed when he said, "There's this guy who won't leave me alone."

Robert's mom found a reason to disappear from the room and give us space. I pointed to her vacated stool, he sat down and I said, "What's going on?" Admittedly, I have no idea what it's like to be fifteen, let alone a boy being pursued by another boy. But I love this kid and I want to be whatever help I can be.

"It's stupid, really. But he won't leave me alone. I don't want to tell him off, but he's constantly making suggestive jokes and he says things about me that just aren't true. He's trying to make something real that isn't," Robert said.

Robert faces challenges I did not face and much of his life is lived in the digital world. I found out just how much in answer to my next question: "Can you tell me what kinds of things he's saying?"

"No, but I can show you," Robert offered as he pulled out his iPhone.

What I silently read was a series of public social media posts by the boy. An outsider would not know the person at the center of the musings was Robert, but he knew. How was I going to bring the Christian worldview to bear for this precious young man? How was I going to help equip him to live authentically as a joyful, theatrical, smart, cisgender man in a sexually confused world? I prayed even as I spoke.

"Robert, let me tell you what I know about you. I know you are a person who is made in God's image, fearfully and wonderfully made. I know that since you were you a little boy you've loved to act. You like rules and boundaries because they provide you the freedom to completely be yourself within bounds. You're intelligent and interesting and in three years you're going to college and four years after that you're probably going to Broadway. You may well be the only Christian there. So, what you're learning to deal with today, with this one boy, may be the preparation you'll need to live faithfully in that environment."

He smiled and I let the silence lengthen.

Finally he said, "Here's what I don't get. He knows I'm not gay. He knows you can't make people gay and yet he won't leave me alone. What's up with that?"

I said, "Wow, you seem to see the situation pretty clearly. I don't know this other boy, but I know you and it sounds like you're being both gracious and truthful, which is all anyone can ask. If you could write the script, what would happen in the story with this boy?"

He answered immediately; he'd clearly thought about it. "He'd be himself and let me be myself and it wouldn't be weird."

"Well," I said, "that's how I'll pray, with you and for you"—and then I did, right there and then. And this big man-child hugged me maybe more for listening than for anything else. Was the issue resolved? No. But Robert was heard and the door to future conversations was left open.

You can do this. You can engage in the conversations of the day in a way that honors Jesus. You can lay claim to a vision for the future beyond the current circumstance. You can uphold the Truth of God's Word and the Grace of God's character and speak with authority into the lives of other people. If God's got you then you've got this.

The issue is marriage and the need for it to be redeemed

I met Sarah at church. Like many conservative Christian women in their thirties, she had not planned to be single at this stage of life. She is petite and beautiful and well educated and very much wants to be married and raising kids. And yet, she's not. A mutual friend suggested I might be an encouragement since I didn't marry until well into my forties. So, one Sunday, I invited Sarah to join our family for lunch after worship. We had a great time getting to know her. She said she'd follow up on getting together with me but never did.

I became aware that others had a growing concern for her obsession with getting married. So, one Sunday I made a point to seek her out after worship. She sat in the pew in front of me and started to gush about the latest failed relationship. I listened to the monologue for several minutes and then firmly said, "Sarah, stop." She didn't so I repeated the command, "Stop. Sarah, stop." Her mouth still agape, she stopped mid-sentence and stared at me.

"I don't think you realize what you're doing so I'm going to challenge you to stop and think about what you're thinking about." She just stared at me.

"Seriously, what is going on in your mind right now? What are you thinking about?"

She said his name and I said, "Why? Why are your thoughts dwelling on him? Let me ask you another question. What was the sermon text today?"

She searched her mind and then allowed her gaze to fall into her lap. She had no idea.

"Okay," I said, "I'm warning you in advance this is going to be very direct, but you need it. You have to stop. You have to stop fixating on every single man who crosses your path. You have to stop pining for the ones who are gone and you have to stop fantasizing on the ones who may be ahead."

I paused but not for long, then I continued, "Do you trust God?" "Yes!" she insisted with a level of passion that surprised me. I smiled.

"Good, let's start with that. If you trust God, do you trust God knows the plans He has for you? And do you trust that those plans are for your welfare and not for harm to give you a hope-filled future?"

Sarah, who happens to be a preacher's kid almost rolled her eyes when she identified, "Jeremiah 29:11."

"Right, but do you believe it for you?" I pressed.

"Yes," she said, but much less enthusiastically—which I pointed out to her.

"Sarah, what kind of man do you hope to marry?"

She had given this a lot of thought and rattled off quite a list in response. When she was done I asked, "And what kind of woman is that kind of man hoping to marry?"

Her answer didn't require words. So I backed off and told a story about my own experience and then observed that the world is very confused about marriage right now. She agreed and we had a good conversation about the need for marriage to be redeemed in our culture and the unique opportunity the Church has to enter into that cultural conversation as the Bride of Christ.

"What might that look like?" I asked.

Energized, she replied, "The Church, as the Bride of Christ, could begin inviting people to meet the bridegroom."

The banter from there was encouraging and uplifting and Sarah exited the conversation with Jesus on her mind instead of whatever his name was who dumped her last. Was her perceived singleness-problem solved? No, but her focus was shifted and sometimes that's the best you can you hope to accomplish. Remember, it's just one conversation. Pray to God for guidance toward the conversation that will follow on the heels of this one.

The issue is life and death

Margaret was dying. Lisa was a nurse in a facility where death is a regular visitor. Lisa knows the signs, the smells, and the sounds that attend death's approach. She knows when a body is not long for this world. Margaret was well loved and aged. Her body was failing and she wanted nothing more than to die in peace. Her children were desperately determined to keep her alive. I was sitting in a coffee shop with Lisa as she vented her frustration.

"They won't let her go. All she wants to do is die and they won't let her go." She was sad and angry and frustrated and physically pained for this sweet dear soul whose physical needs she'd been tending to for months.

I listened. Silently. Compassionately. Attentively to this young woman who tirelessly tends to the needs of the dying during the day, and then on Sunday and Wednesday evenings, she shepherds the hearts of teenage girls in a church discipleship group. Eventually her recitation came to an exhausted conclusion and she sat quietly with her shoulders slumped toward the table between us. Only then did I speak.

"Lisa, you've told me what Margaret wants. You've told me what her family wants. You've told me what you want for her. What do you think God wants?" I asked gently and slowly and with compassion for all involved.

"I don't know. I haven't even thought about that," she answered through moist eyes that never left the now tepid cup of coffee in her hands.

"You and I both know God is sovereign over life and death. He loves Margaret. He has loved Margaret since before the foundations of the earth. He lovingly knit her together in her mother's womb eighty-four years ago. He loves her more than you do. He loves her more than her family. I know it seems like people here are keeping her alive, but you and I both know God has the power to take her to Himself whenever He chooses." I paused and then gently continued, "God also has the power to use her remaining life to do something that may yet not be done. Maybe this isn't about Margaret." And then I asked Lisa to tell me about the members of Margaret's family.

It was as if the light had come on. Lisa is a sensitive Christian, but she'd been so focused on the person who was dying she missed some things about the living people cycling in and out of the room. She sat up straight, looked me in the eye and spoke with great clarity, "I know exactly who this is about. It's about her grandson, Chad. He's sullen. He even seems afraid of her. But he's there every night. He comes and goes in the dark. He rarely speaks to anyone. He just sits in the chair in the corner of her room and listens to her breathe. You can hear him crying."

It was as if Lisa had found the mission in the midst of the misery. "Ok," I said, "so, it's Chad. What are you going to ask Chad when you see him tonight?"

Lisa didn't hesitate to answer, "I'm going to ask him if he's crying because he's sad or if he's crying because he's scared or for some other reason."

She did and you know what? Chad was afraid. He wasn't afraid of the machines or the shell of the person who used to be his grandma disappearing into the folds of the sheets. He was afraid he would never see his Mima again. Lisa recalled their conversation to me. She asked her question about fear and Chad answered with a question of his own, "Everyone is talking like she's just moving next door. But death is death and that's it. There isn't anything else, right?"

Lisa told me with that she pulled a stool over next to Chad and sat down. She told him death was not as final as some people think, but she wanted to know more about Mima. Lisa got Chad talking about Margaret and periodically he mentioned her church. Lisa didn't know Margaret before she'd been too weak to really talk. The family had Margaret transferred from the hospital in her hometown to this facility so no pastor or church people had been to see her. Lisa asked Chad if he'd ever talked with his grandma about why she went to church or what she did there. He had not.

Lisa said, let's try something. And she scooted over to Margaret's bedside. Lisa started to hum Amazing Grace and Margaret, who to that point had seemed unconscious, raised her brow slightly and started to hum along. Lisa then started to sing the words and Margaret's frail lips moved with the song. There was no volume but she was singing.

Chad drew closer to his grandmother than he had in weeks. He carefully took her fragile hand in his own as tears streamed down his cheeks. He looked from Margaret to Lisa and back again as the women sang this strange song. Finally he said, "Grandma, when you die you're going to heaven but I don't know how to get there. So I'll never see you again!" The young man sobbed.

At this Margaret opened her eyes, squeezed his hand, looked to Lisa and spoke her last two words in this life, "Tell him."

Lisa did just that and by His grace, God took Margaret to Himself that night.

The issue is criminal justice and incarceration and second chances

I had one too many things to manage as I exited the cab in front of the Union Rescue Mission in D.C. I was going from the meeting to the airport and hadn't really thought it might look like I was moving in. The men who live at the rescue mission had obviously been told that some group of suits was holding a meeting in the building so they were out front and immediately motioned to the left side of the building where I was supposed to be. The problem was I was early, had a coffee to drink, and was far more interested in the guys sitting out front than in the pre-meeting chit-chat taking place inside. So, I ignored their directions and rolled my suitcase into the concrete courtyard. Two gentlemen were sitting at a table and once I caught their eye I maneuvered toward them.

"May I join you for coffee?" I asked.

They motioned to an empty seat, looking warily at me. They each had a cup of coffee and there was a folded newspaper in the center of the table.

I introduced myself and offered my hand, which was apparently a somewhat unusual gesture as both guys awkwardly shook my hand as they told me their names.

"Elmer and Rick, it's nice to meet you. Thanks for letting me share your table. Don't let me interrupt your conversation. What were you talking about before I intruded?" I asked.

"Him," was the one word answer as the man to my right flipped the paper open to reveal a picture of Donald Trump. With that we were off.

"What do you think about him?" I asked. Their answers were colorful.

"But she's just as bad," the man across from me said as the conversation turned from Trump to Clinton.

It occurred to me that at that moment I could have been sitting with any two people at any table over coffee in any city, town, or hamlet in America. We were just three citizens talking about the challenges we face as a nation.

Then my ignorance came to the fore, "So, who are you going to vote for?" My question was met with silence and I saw their jaws tighten and their faces slightly harden.

Elmer looked at the paper in the middle of the table as he said, "Ma'am, we don't get to vote no more."

I didn't answer until he raised his eyes. I looked at him and said, "Elmer, I'm so sorry. I had no intention of embarrassing you. I didn't know."

Rick bailed me out, "It's alright. How could you? But that's why we're here. It's hard to get started again once you've been on the inside."

The conversation turned to jobs and the lack of them. And then Elmer said something I'll never forget, "The world changed a lot in the twelve years I was in. But the world don't give me no credit for all the ways I changed."

He's right and that's wrong. We all three agreed Christians ought to be on the forefront of criminal justice reform and that churches ought to be helping people who have done their time and paid their debt to society and are actually living a redeemed life. To that point Rick said, "Jesus is all about second chances. And more than that if a person needs it. Look at Peter. He messed up a lot but Jesus kept giving him another chance. People could learn from that."

Yes, Rick and Elmer, indeed we could.

Whether the issue is pancakes, porcupines, politics, or parenting, the issue is God. "What?" you ask. Yes, really. From the subject of pancakes, you can talk about manna, bread of heaven, and from there the bread of life, Jesus Christ. From the subject of porcupines, you can talk about how to love prickly people and the defenses we put around our hearts that keep us from deeply experiencing the love of God. Politics provides endless fodder for conversation because politics is just a fancy word for all the activities associated with the governance of people. People are both precious and problematic—that's a summary of creation and the fall. How fallen people manage themselves in community is the question that politicians are always trying to answer. Parenting encompasses every issue under heaven because our children are not only a sacred trust but also our brothers and sisters in Christ. Helping them grow up in every way into Christ as the head is our primary parental calling.

Feeling alliterate? Consider how you would reconnect the eternal with the everyday using words associated with any letter of the alphabet. Write a phrase next to each word that connects the eternal to these very everyday things:

- Ambulance, art, awake
- Beauty, babble, battery
- Center, character, crack
- Yes, yo-yo, Yield sign

I like to copy the text from an article and paste it into Wordle.com and then use it as a discussion starter. Or see what's trending on Google or Twitter and then literally start a conversation with someone.

I know what you're thinking, "What would someone think if I did that?"

Newsflash: most people are not thinking at all which is why they answer "nothin," when you ask them what they're thinking about. Second newsflash: if they are thinking about something, it's not you. Our goal is to fill that empty space with a perspective they may not have considered about whatever is in front of them.

Every conversation is about God because God is always the issue. Life, death, taxes, dating, marriage, work, worth, money, sex, power—God cares about all of it because God cares about the people affected by it.

What would happen to our conversations if we entered every encounter with another person—every encounter—as a potential divine appointment God set for that day? What if our eyes were continually scanning the environment for people in need of encouragement, blessing, hope, help, or a simple smile? What might happen if we cast the seed of God's love as lavishly as the sower who went out to sow?

If you find yourself in line, look around.

If you find yourself stuck in traffic, look around.

If you find yourself sitting alone in a coffee shop, look around.

If you find yourself in a rain delay at a baseball game, look around.

If you find yourself in the surgical waiting room, look around.

If you find yourself in a new part of town, look around.

If you find yourself in a new cultural moment, look around.

Jesus had the Father's eyes and He also shared the Father's will and Spirit. He had the Kingdom of God at the forefront of His mind at all times. He was never lost and He showed people the Way even when they didn't know they were looking.

The woman at the well in John 4 is just one illustration of how we can follow Jesus' lead into conversations with people who are living in ways we don't approve, from parts of town we don't like, and where the result is redemption not damnation. Isn't that what we really want? (That's a gut check question. When you see a prostitute or a gang-banger or a refugee or an immigrant or a homeless person or a mentally ill person who is a disheveled mess, what do you really want in your heart of hearts? Jesus wants redemption.)

Look around. Instead of answering the question "What do I see?" answer the question "Who do I see?"

Invariably "what" you will see is a mess. But in the midst of all that mess are precious people, children of God, made in His image, whose redemption God intends. And YOU are the agent of grace present at this very moment sharing the same patch of real estate. If this were a game of tag I'd be saying, "You're it!"

QUESTIONS FOR PERSONAL REFLECTION AND GROUP DISCUSSION

1. Which section of the news do you turn to or click on first? Why?
2. Choose a headline from your newsfeed and just practice finding the God angle. Where is the hook that reconnects the mundane to the miraculous? What does the story say about life, death, humanity, love, justice, sin, forgiveness, or what Biblical allusion is hiding in plain sight?
3. Practice connecting the eternal with the everyday using literally ANY word, object, or event. How does this reflect (accurately or inaccurately) Creation, the Redemptive arc of history, God's glory, or the reality of Sin?
4. Which of the stories in this chapter stands out to you: Liza, Robert, Sarah, Lisa, Elmer, or Rick, and why? What story do you want to add?

Reentering the Conversation, Reengaging the Culture, Reconnecting the Eternal with the Everyday

This is a Moment of Truth in America. The battle for Truth has never been more public and the battle lines have rarely been so clear. The issues appear to be myriad but they can be distilled to one very simple question: is it the Truth?

Jesus is the Way and the Truth and the Life. For Christians there is not an alternative to telling the Truth and bearing witness to the Truth in all circumstances. Does it get us into trouble in this world? Sometimes, but to do anything other than Speak the Truth is to betray the very One whose name we bear.

Here are a few reminders of the markers of Truth:

If it is not consistent with the reality of who God is, it is not true.

If it is not good, it is not true.

If it is not beautiful, it is not true.

If it does not advance the Gospel, God's great redemptive plan in Jesus Christ, it is not true.

It may feel true. We might wish it were true. It may sound good. But if it is not true then it's simply not an option.

For each of us there are moments of truth every day. Life is full of them.

The question from the backseat.

The diagnosis from the doctor.

The pink-slip or termination letter.

The knock at the door in the middle of the night.

There is a scene in Charles Dickens' *A Christmas Carol* when the spirit of Christmas past is reminding Ebenezer Scrooge of how he responded to the moments of truth in his life. As a young man there is a scene with his Belle, his fiancée, that changes the course of all that follows.

From Stave 2: The First of the Three Spirits:

> There was an eager, greedy, restless motion in the eye, which showed the passion that had taken root, and where the shadow of the growing tree would fall.
>
> He was not alone, but sat by the side of a fair young girl in a mourning-dress: in whose eyes there were tears, which sparkled in the light that shone out of the Ghost of Christmas Past.
>
> "It matters little," she said, softly. "To you, very little. Another idol has displaced me; and if it can cheer and comfort you in time to come, as I would have tried to do, I have no just cause to grieve."
>
> "What Idol has displaced you?" he rejoined.
>
> "A golden one."

"This is the even-handed dealing of the world!" he said. "There is nothing on which it is so hard as poverty; and there is nothing it professes to condemn with such severity as the pursuit of wealth!"

"You fear the world too much," she answered, gently. "All your other hopes have merged into the hope of being beyond the chance of its sordid reproach. I have seen your nobler aspirations fall off one by one, until the master-passion, Gain, engrosses you. Have I not?"

"What then?" he retorted. "Even if I have grown so much wiser, what then? I am not changed towards you."

She shook her head.

"Am I?"

"Our contract is an old one. It was made when we were both poor and content to be so, until, in good season, we could improve our worldly fortune by our patient industry. You are changed. When it was made, you were another man."

"I was a boy," he said impatiently.

"Your own feeling tells you that you were not what you are," she returned. "I am. That which promised happiness when we were one in heart, is fraught with misery now that we are two. How often and how keenly I have thought of this, I will not say. It is enough that I have thought of it, and can release you."

"Have I ever sought release?"

"In words? No. Never."

"In what, then?"

"In a changed nature; in an altered spirit; in another atmosphere of life; another Hope as its great end. In every-thing that made my love of any worth or value in your sight. If this had never been between us," said the girl, looking mildly, but with steadiness, upon him; "tell me, would you seek me out and try to win me now? Ah, no!"

He seemed to yield to the justice of this supposition, in spite of himself. But he said with a struggle," You think not?"

"I would gladly think otherwise if I could," she answered, "Heaven knows. When I have learned a Truth like this, I know how strong and irresistible it must be. But if you were free to-day, to-morrow, yesterday, can even I believe that you would choose a dowerless girl—you who, in your very confidence with her, weigh everything by Gain: or, choosing her, if for a moment you were false enough to your one guiding principle to do so, do I not know that your repentance and regret would surely follow? I do; and I release you. With a full heart, for the love of him you once were."

He was about to speak; but with her head turned from him, she resumed.

"You may—the memory of what is past half makes me hope you will—have pain in this. A very, very brief time, and you will dismiss the recollection of it, gladly, as an unprofitable dream, from which it happened well that you awoke. May you be happy in the life you have chosen."

She left him, and they parted.[1]

Scrooge was, most certainly, not happy in the life he chose.

This scene, in fact *A Christmas Carol* in its entirety, reminds us that we face moments of truth where we can choose right or wrong, good or evil, life and death. And how we respond in those moments changes us. Our responses impact the world around us and they change the course of events in the world. Yes, Ebenezer Scrooge is, as a man, who he was when he was left to spend holidays alone at boarding school. But as a man, he made choices in moments in time that powerfully affected not only his own life but the life of others around him.

As he looks back at the moment he allowed Belle to walk out of his life, we see that throughout Belle remains consistently the character she was. It was Scrooge who changed. And in the moment of truth when we all hope he would rise and go after her, rejecting the idols of the world for the truth of real love, he opts for the pursuit of wealth and follows a path that grows ever darker.

Dickens uses powerful images and words to speak the truth. Do we? Do we call out those we love for what they are? Do we call idolatry what it is? Do we point out to them just how much they have changed in pursuit of that which does not ultimately satisfy? Do we know ourselves as well as Belle knew herself and do we see others as clearly as she saw her once beloved Scrooge?

Times change and yes, people change, but as Dickens points out, "I am" remains.

Big moments of truth, like this pivotal moment with Belle, come only a few times in a given life. But smaller moments of truth, like opening the door to a child singing a carol, come quite frequently. We know the dramatic testimonies of Moses at the burning bush and Paul on the road to Damascus, Daniel facing the prospect of the lion's den, Mary's visit from the angel Gabriel, and Jesus in the Garden of Gethsemane. Each faced a moment of truth. But most of life is far more mundane, routine, and, yes, conversational.

There's a moment of truth when we're standing in line and the person in front of us doesn't have quite enough to pay for what they need. There's a moment of truth when traffic is snarled and our response is a testimony to those in the backseat and all around us on the road. There's a moment of truth every time we don't get exactly what we ordered in a restaurant. There's a moment of truth when the options on the TV screen list everything from that which is rated G to XXX. There's a moment of truth every time we log on to the internet. There's a moment of truth when the phone rings, the milk is spilled, the tire is flat, the rain falls, the rent is due, the pressure rises, the alarm rings. In this moment of truth, who will I be? How will I respond? What spirit will be revealed? What words will I speak? Which kingdom will I represent?

Every moment is a moment of truth. No, not the dramatic "everything hangs on this decision, hinge of history" kind of moment of truth, but a moment of truth nonetheless. In this very moment, is your mind conformed to the mind of Christ? In this moment, does your heart belong to God? In this moment, are you ready and willing to follow the Spirit's lead?

This is your moment and this is a moment of truth!

So, go, as an ambassador of God's Kingdom perspective, speaking the mind of Christ on the matters of the day. Whatever else today may be, this is the day the Lord has made. And the Lord sends you to be His agent of grace, a living demonstration of the Gospel in it.

You're ready, the divine appointments are set, so go!

Keep the conversation going at
www.carmenfowlerlaberge.com

Appendix

Notes for book club or small group leaders: Conversation starters and tips are offered for adapting the content of the book for use in book club or small group settings.

Organizing your discussion:

There's an old adage that says, "Prepare as if everything depends on you and pray as if everything depends on God." This I know, you can only lead others as deep or as far as you yourself have gone. So, number one, read the entire book in advance, make marginal notes, and pray for those who will participate in the group. For the final session of your group you'll need a physical copy of the newspaper. Have people bring a paper with them—the wider the variety the better. And for your "online only" folks, have them bring their e-reader.

Use the questions within each chapter and at the end of each chapter to provoke conversation. Remember, the goal is to equip and activate Christians so the more you can bring that to the fore the more effective this exercise will be.

The role of prayer and your role as a prayerful leader cannot be overemphasized. There are many times when all we can do is pray, confident that God has it all and has us in the midst of it all. Lead your people into prayer if you are unable to lead them anywhere else!

Discussing the book over twelve weeks:

For the first several weeks keep a running list of questions people want to address in real conversations. You're not putting them off so much as allowing everyone to get far enough along in the book that practical application makes sense and proves effective in actually bringing the mind of Christ to bear on the matters of the day.

Week 1: Introduction & Conclusion (beginning with the end in mind)

Week 2: Chapter 1

Week 3: Chapter 2

Week 4: Chapter 3

Week 5: Chapter 4

Week 6: Chapter 5

Week 7: Chapter 6 and getting personal

Week 8: Chapter 7 and practical practice

Week 9: Chapter 8 and practical practice

Week 10: Chapter 9 and practical practice

Week 11: Chapter 10 and practical practice

Week 12: Conclusion and practical practice

Discussing the book over four weeks or in a retreat setting with four sessions:

This discussion format assumes participants have read the entire book prior to the start of the conversation. You will need to plan to summarize large sections of text, open the conversation to participant observations and "aha" moments, and then use selective questions from the chapters you're covering to stimulate conversation.

Week 1: Premise & Conclusion

Week 2: Part I, Chapters 1–5

Week 3: Part 2, Chapters 6–10

Week 4: Practical practice (you will need physical copies of a newspaper)

Discussing the entire book in a two-hour event, like a monthly book club.

The best you can do is hit the high notes. Focus on the introduction and chapter ten.

From the chapters, highlight:

- God belongs in the middle of every conversation. Why isn't that happening?
- What's the difference between giving people a piece of our mind and giving them the peace of the mind of Christ?
- Are you trying to hold it all together? How is that working for you? What does it mean to accept Jesus as the integrating reality of our lives?
- Until the Word of God is restored to its rightful place in the life of the Church, the Church cannot take her

rightful place in the life of the culture. What does that mean?

- Do you take the Gospel personally? What does that mean?
- Where do I know I'm failing to acknowledge God always in all ways?
- How can I focus less on what's wrong with the world and more on what's right with God?
- Which contestant in the Miss Representation pageant did you associate with?
- What's one thing that breaks the heart of God that breaks my heart? How can I make the world different on that one issue?
- "Jesus doesn't speak to issues, Jesus spoke to people." Do you see the difference?
- God needs to be put in His place—back in the middle of every conversation—and you're just the person to do it! How can you start today?

Acknowledgments

H ere at the close of this book I want to acknowledge with deepest gratitude the people who have influenced my life and those who now surround me in ministry. No one writes a book—or puts together a radio show or even gets dinner on the table every night—on their own. From the echoes of my mother's proclamations that "you may be the only Bible other people read today," to my sister and best friend's encouragement that more people need to hear the unique tone of voice I bring to the issues of the day, I am grateful. So, here goes, in an effort to leave no one out and yet knowing that I will: thank you to the Benefiel and Fowler families, to my sister Tiana, and BFF Jessica, to Roxmere Road neighbors and Tampa Bay Little League friends, Mrs. Mabry and Coach Fife, the McWhirters, Stichters, Wichmans, and Marcy (some people transcend last names); to Kathy Conner, Robert and Virginia Morris, and everyone else in YoungLife; Tom Gillespie, Marnie Crumpler, Tom Edwards, Connie Wood, Darwin and Mary Koenning, David Peterson, the Vollmers, Grists, and people of Rabun County, Georgia; Howard and Trisha Edington, Paige Ragan, David Swanson, Luder Whitlock, and the people of Orlando; Jack and Verena Bruner, Jeff Jeremiah, Dean Weaver, Gerrit Dawson, Parker and Patty Williamson, Paula Kincaid, and the members of the Presbyterian Lay Committee board and staff; Joe Battaglia, Chris Gould, and Marji Ross—we wouldn't be here without you; and to the Regnery Faith and Reconnect teams—especially Jon Wilke, Amanda Duvall, Jen Lee, Lisa Wilson, Lynn Simpson, and Gary Terashita, thank you all. You each know the part you have played in the Gospel advance in my life. You are precious to me and without you I fully acknowledge I would not be where I am today, doing what I love: seeking to equip the people of God to get off the sidelines and bring God back into the conversations of the day in ways that honor Jesus. Ultimately, all gratitude goes to God and I acknowledge full well that apart from His all-sufficient grace, none of this would be possible.

Finally, to my precious husband, Jim … words fail and tears of gratitude don't take well to the printed page. So, let me simply affirm, "I am with you, all the way home." Oh, and Susan Andrews, save me a seat!

Notes

Introduction

1. "U.S. Public Becoming Less Religious," Pew Research Center, November 3, 2015, http://www.pewforum.org/2015/11/03/u-s-public-becoming-less-religious/.
2. "Groundbreaking ACFI Survey Reveals How Many Adults Have a Biblical Worldview," American Culture & Faith Institute, February 27, 2017, https://www.culturefaith.com/groundbreaking-survey-by-acfi-reveals-how-many-american-adults-have-a-biblical-worldview/.
3. "Leading in a Pluralistic Society," Q Research Brief, http://qideas.org/QResearchBrief.pdf.
4. Ibid.
5. Anna Bartlett Warner (1827–1915).

6.   But how do we know the mind of Christ? Even the church seems confused about what the Bible says. We could quote seminary professors who would lead us to believe diametrically opposed things about who God is, what God has said, what God wants, and where history is headed. Some of them are right and some of them are wrong—that's been the reality since the first generation when Peter, Paul, and Jude warn against false teaching. We have to discern the truth from falsehood and we cannot rely on professional clergy to tell us what to believe.

So, how do you know if your pastor is teaching the truth or actively suppressing the truth? How do you discern between teaching submitted to God's will versus that which is advocating the will of man?

Here's a quick litmus test of where your pastor stands in terms of the authority of the Bible. What do they say about the Bible and sermon immediately before they preach or teach? Do they invite you to "listen for the Word of God" or do they invite you to "listen to the Word of God?" It may seem irrelevant, but there's a vast theological chasm between "for" and "to." Listening for the word of God suggests not everything about to be read from the Bible is, in point of fact, the word of God. Those listening are the judge of what is and isn't to be considered God's word. Listening for God's word also suggests God might speak something through the sermon that doesn't appear in the Bible, but a word God might be speaking in new revelation through the preacher today.

Contrast that with the invitation to listen "to" the Word of God. That is a declaration that everything we are about to hear from the Bible is the very Word of God. We may or may not fully understand it and it may be hard to hear, but that does not change the reality God has said it and we must deal with it. Listening "to" the Word of God also puts us in the right receptive posture. God has spoken and God will now speak, by the power of the Holy Spirit, through the fully submitted life of the preacher. At any point the person talking departs from the Word God has spoken, that person is in error—not the other way around.

Chapter 1

1. Megan Specia and Maher Samaan, "Syrian Boy Who Became Image of Civil War Reappears," *New York Times*, June 6, 2017, https://www. nytimes.com/2017/06/06/world/middleeast/omran-daqneesh-syria-aleppo.html?mcubz=0.

2. Laura Jesson, "I'm Scared to Come Out: Here's Why I'm Doing It.," *Sojourners* (September 2016), https://sojo.net/articles/im-scared-come-out-heres-why-im-doing-it.

3. Ibid.

4. Ibid.

5. Ibid.

6. "2016 State of American Theology Study," Lifeway Research (2016): 17, https://thestateoftheology.com/assets/downloads/2016-state-of-america-white-paper.pdf.

Chapter 2

1. Laura Jesson, "I'm Scared to Come Out: Here's Why I'm Doing It.," *Sojourners* (September 2016), https://sojo.net/articles/im-scared-come-out-heres-why-im-doing-it.

2. Ibid.

3. Bob Smietana, "Research: Unchurched Will Talk about Faith, Not Interested in Going to Church," LifeWay, June 28, 2016, http://blog. lifeway.com/newsroom/2016/06/28/research-unchurched-will-talk-about-faith-not-interested-in-going-to-church/.

Chapter 3

1. Peter Singer and Karen Dawn, "Harambe the Gorilla Dies, Meat-Eaters Grieve," *Los Angeles Times*, June 5, 2016, www.latimes.com/opinion/op-ed/la-oe-singer-dawn-harambe-death-zoo-20160605-snap-story.html.

2. Belinda Luscombe, "Porn and the Threat to Virility," *Time*, March 31, 2016, http://time.com/4277510/porn-and-the-threat-to-virility/.

3. Judith Shulevitz, "It's O.K., Liberal Parents, You Can Freak Out about Porn," *New York Times* (July 16, 2016), https://www.nytimes.com/2016/07/17/opinion/sunday/its-ok-liberal-parents-you-can-freak-out-about-porn.html.

4. "Investigative Footage," The Center for Medical Progress, http://www.centerformedicalprogress.org/cmp/investigative-footage/.

5. "Meet the Press—April 3, 2016," NBC News (April 3, 2016), https://www.nbcnews.com/meet-the-press/meet-press-april-3-2016-n549916.

6. "Personal Journey: Emma Is a Boy," *The Atlanta Journal-Constitution*, http://www.myajc.com/videos/news/personal-journey-emma-is-a-boy/vDrM9f/.

Chapter 4

1. The Covenant Network of Presbyterians "Marriage Matters" conference at Fourth Presbyterian Church, Chicago, Illinois, 2013, http://covnetpres.org/2013-covenant-conference-marriage-matters/.

2. http://www.americandialect.org/2015-word-of-the-year-is-singular-they; https://en.oxforddictionaries.com/definition/us/they.

3. Jacob Tobia, "Everything You Ever Wanted to Know about Gender-Neutral Pronouns," *Motto*, May 12, 2016, http://motto.time.com/4327915/gender-neutral-pronouns/.

4. See Andrea Casteel Smith, *Scarred Beautiful: My True Story of Finding God in Despair and Beauty in Imperfection* (Denver: Outskirts Press, 2015).

Chapter 5

1. Pew Research, America's Changing Religious Landscape, 2015, http://www.pewforum.org/2015/05/12/chapter-1-the-changing-religious-composition-of-the-u-s/.

2. "What We Believe," United Chruch of Christ website, accessed on July 28, 2017, www.ucc.org/about-us_what-we-believe.

3. Interview with Lori Koch, "Is the Bible Still Visible in Public Life," *Reconnect One, The Reconnect with Carmen LaBerge*, September 16, 2016, https://reconnectwithcarmen.com/share-good-news-anyone-language/.

4. C.S. Lewis, *The Abolition of Man*: Reflections on education with special reference to the teaching of English in the upper forms of schools, Oxford University Press 1943, Chapter 1: Men without chests.

5. Kathy Bright, "There's Nothing Wrong with Racism...," Kathy Bright's Korner, February 26, 2011, http://blog.dg4kids.com/kathy-brights-korner/there%E2%80%99s-nothing-wrong-with-racism%E2%80%A6/.

Chapter 6
1. "Spotlight Interview: Jone Eareckson Tada on How to Respond to 'Right to Die,'" *The Reconnect with Carmen LaBerge*, December 5, 2016, https://reconnectwithcarmen.com/spotlight-interview-joni-eareckson-tada-respond-right-die/.

Chapter 7
1. http://bibleapps.com/ephesians/4-25.htm.

Chapter 8
1. Francis Schaeffer, *He Is There and He Is Not Silent* (Carol Stream, IL: Tyndale House Publishers, Inc., 2001).

Conclusion
1. Charles Dickens, *A Christmas Carol* (New York: Dover Publications, 1991).

Index